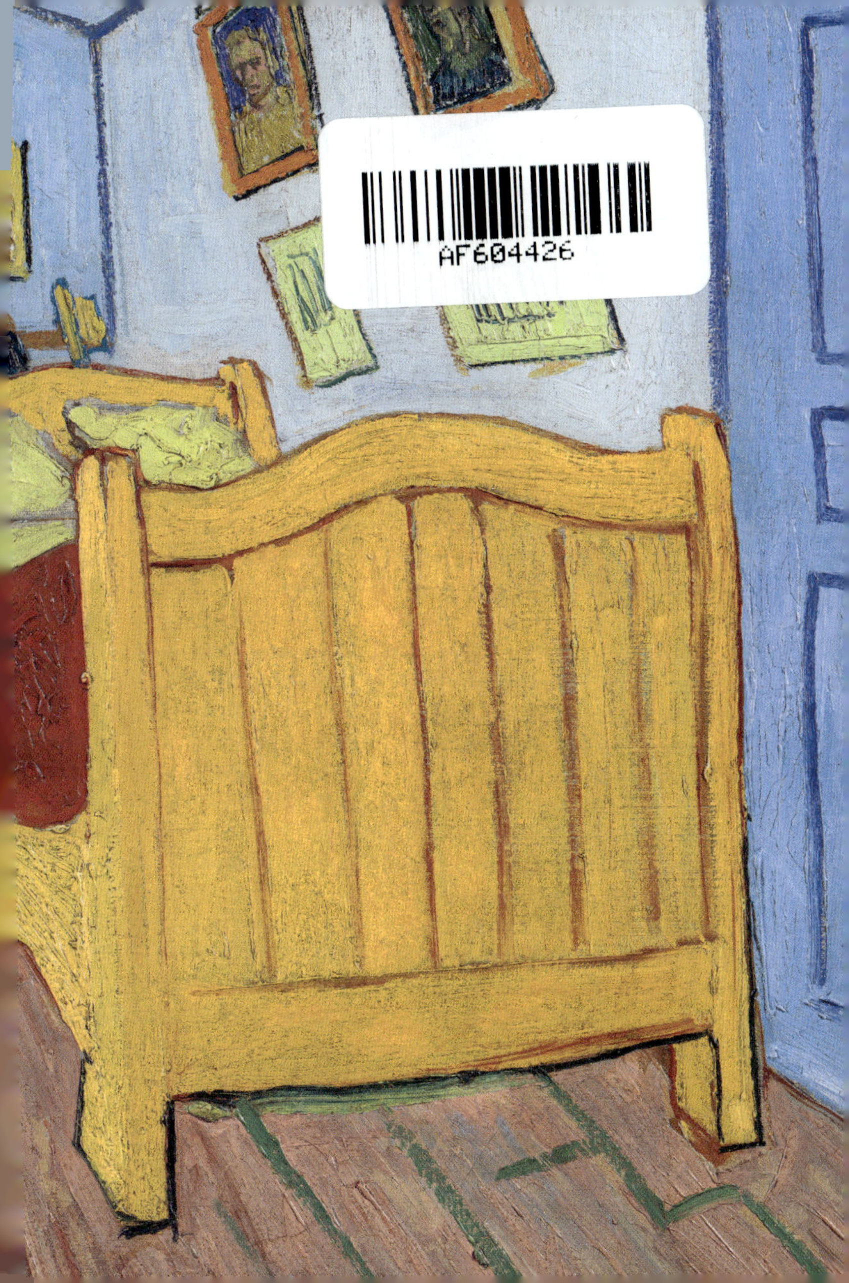

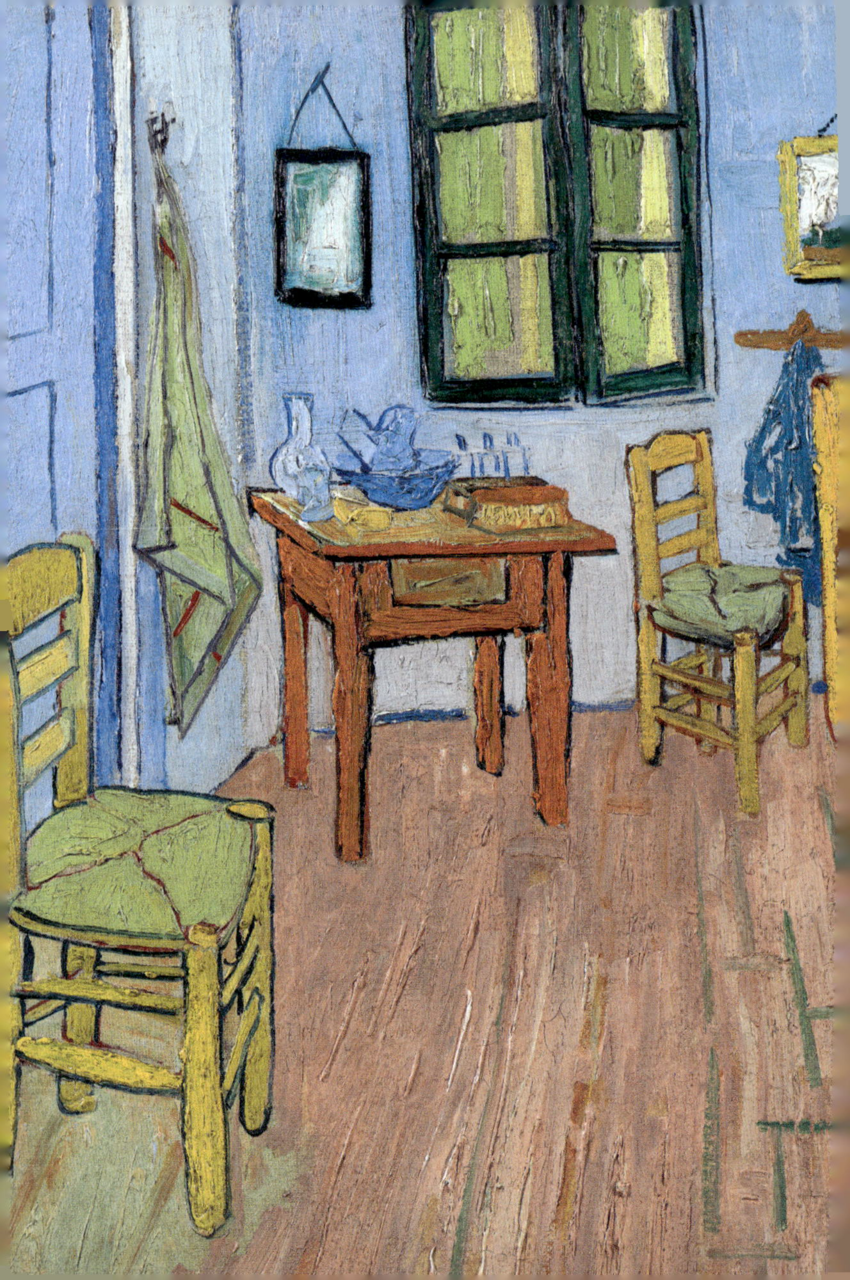

Find things beautiful as much
as you can, most people
find too little beautiful.

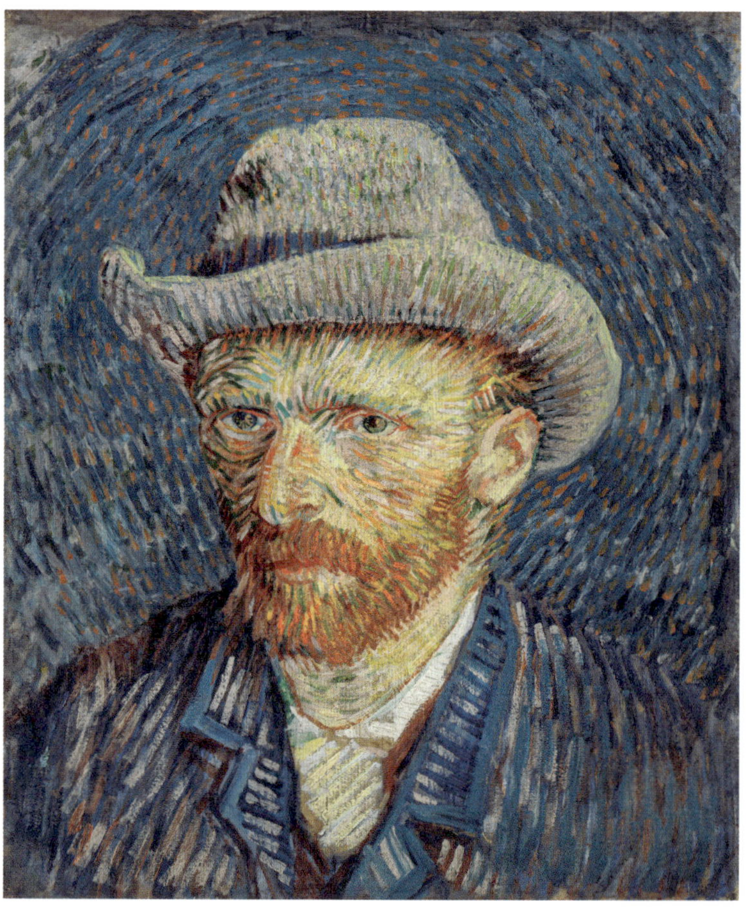

THE WORLD ACCORDING TO

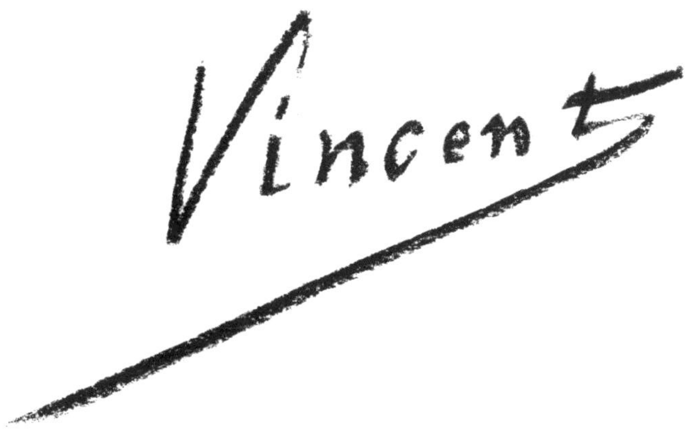

Edited by
Nienke Bakker
& Ann Blokland

with 64 illustrations

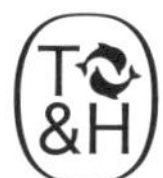

First published in the United Kingdom in 2024 by
Thames & Hudson Ltd, 181A High Holborn, London WC1V 7QX

First published in the United States of America in 2024 by
Thames & Hudson Inc., 500 Fifth Avenue, New York, New York 10110

British Library Cataloguing-in-Publication Data
A catalogue record for this book is available from the British Library

Library of Congress Control Number 2024934763

ISBN 978-0-500-02872-8

Printed and bound in China by C&C Offset Printing Co., Ltd

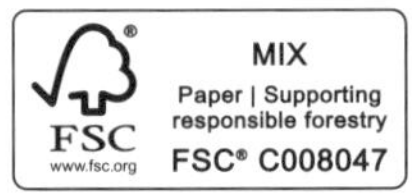

Contents

INTRODUCTION
Letters Full of Life Lessons 7

Van Gogh on Art 12

Van Gogh on Colour 30

Van Gogh on Nature 42

Van Gogh on Ambition 62

Van Gogh on Character 78

Van Gogh on Illness 90

Van Gogh on Sorrow and Consolation 98

Van Gogh on Life 108

Van Gogh on Spirituality 130

Van Gogh on Love and Friendship 150

Van Gogh on the Future 162

SOURCES 172

ILLUSTRATIONS 173

BIOGRAPHY 174

INTRODUCTION

Letters Full of Life Lessons

BY ESTHER DARLEY

'Almost no one knows that the secret of beautiful work is to a large extent good faith and sincere feeling', Vincent van Gogh wrote to his brother Theo in 1882, barely two years after deciding to become an artist. Yet he was already able to pinpoint where the essence of good work came from. 'Good faith and sincere feeling' are also precisely the qualities from which his letters derive their power. Vincent might not have been a natural talent as an artist – he worked and studied ceaselessly to improve his skills – yet the words flowed easily from his pen right from the very beginning. Raised as the son of a Protestant minister, he was instilled with a feeling for language from an early age. 'We must correspond often', he wrote to Theo in 1872 in one of his first letters from The Hague, where he was working at their uncle's art firm. More than 800 of Vincent's letters have survived, the last one written from Auvers-sur-Oise a few days before his death.

Van Gogh wrote regularly to relatives and artist friends, but the vast majority of his letters were addressed to his favourite brother, Theo. Together, they form what is perhaps the most frank and unique body of artists' correspondence ever written. One that offers, moreover, a rare insight into Vincent's mental turmoil and artistic motivations. The fact that his letters still speak to our imagination today not only reflects the fluency of his pen, the lyrical and compelling style of his writing and his ability to structure a letter capable of holding the reader's interest from start to finish; it is also due to the way he pours out his soul, so that we get to know the artist as a human being – a person unable to escape himself who doggedly pursued his goal, even if he was unsure at first quite what that goal might be. His descriptions of everyday concerns are interspersed with highly intense passages, beautiful sentences and wise words on subjects like ambition, love, loneliness and his battle with mental illness. They consist of surprising, melancholy and sometimes very funny comments, which transcend the individual and continue to inspire and console many people today, some 130 years after he wrote them. Just as his paintings do.

Vincent was first and foremost a brilliant observer who penned descriptions – simultaneously sharp and poetic – of the nature that brought him peace and in which he hoped to find God. Nothing seems to have escaped him during his endless walks: from flaming sunsets, singing larks and green-grey stripes in the sea to the trampled grass along the side of the road. As you read, you feel as if you were walking at his side. Yet all the while Vincent's head is working overtime to process the associations that bubble up in him ceaselessly: the grass 'looks tired and dusty like the inhabitants of a poor quarter' while a row of pollard willows suggests 'a procession of orphan men'. It was for good reason then that he advised Theo: 'Always continue walking a lot and loving nature, for that's the real way to learn to understand art better and better.' At first, Vincent's letters to Theo, four years his junior, mainly consist of this kind of advice, as we might expect of an older brother. Later, when Theo had also started work in the art trade, they shared their love of literature ('an irresistible passion'), of music and the works of art they were discovering. When Vincent felt it was his vocation to become a preacher, he immediately began to bombard Theo with moralizing letters exhorting him to stick to the straight and narrow path. Their relationship changed when Vincent decided at the age of 27 to become an artist and Theo began to support him financially. Their correspondence grew more intensive, as Vincent now needed to confirm at regular intervals that he had received his brother's money. Hence the many messages that begin 'thanks for your kind letter and the 50-franc note'. He also felt obliged to keep Theo informed about his progress, occasionally including a 'croquis [sketch] of the latest canvas'. In this way, we learn a great deal about Vincent's way of working and ideas. That he considered the results of the academic method of teaching to be 'flat', 'dead' and 'bloody boring', for instance. Or that he used colour 'more arbitrarily in order to express myself forcefully' and that he would rather paint eyes than cathedrals. But also that 'painting and fucking a lot' were not compatible or that raising children was better than channelling all your energy into painting.

Apart from the honesty of his words, it is worth asking whether Vincent was a good writer because he was able to look so closely and whether his powers of observation improved as he became a better painter. Yet it was not only outwardly that he directed his gaze: as he attempted to get a grip on existence and his own significance within it – 'Life's "an odd thing", brother'– he also turned it inwards, seeking to express in words the deepest fears, doubts and rage that remain invisible. 'What moulting is to birds, the time when they change their feathers, that's adversity or misfortune, hard times, for us human beings', he wrote after suffering his latest setback. It is heart-breaking to read how weighed down he felt by his illness and his fear and doubt that he would ever recover. Yet his words are comforting and encouraging too, since he tried not to despair and to keep going instead. Because 'hoping for better times mustn't be a feeling but a doing something in the present': advice that remains as valuable as ever. We can feel sad about the unfortunate end to Vincent's life while still being energized by his euphoric thoughts on the art of the future, his collaboration with others and painting itself, when – in the good moments – 'my brush goes between my fingers as if it were a bow on the violin'. So it is that his letters generate a new meaning for everyone, differently each time.

We hope that this selection of the most beautiful quotations from Vincent's letters will convey the same kind of recognition and emotion that he sought to achieve with his art. He was eager to reach other people and to mean something to them. But he could never have suspected that through his immense talent for capturing personal experiences, ideas and feelings in evocative and appealing language, he had genuine life lessons to offer us. 'There are so many people [...] who imagine that words are nothing. On the contrary, don't you think, it's as interesting and as difficult to say a thing well as to paint a thing. There's the art of lines and colours, but there's the art of words that will last just the same.'

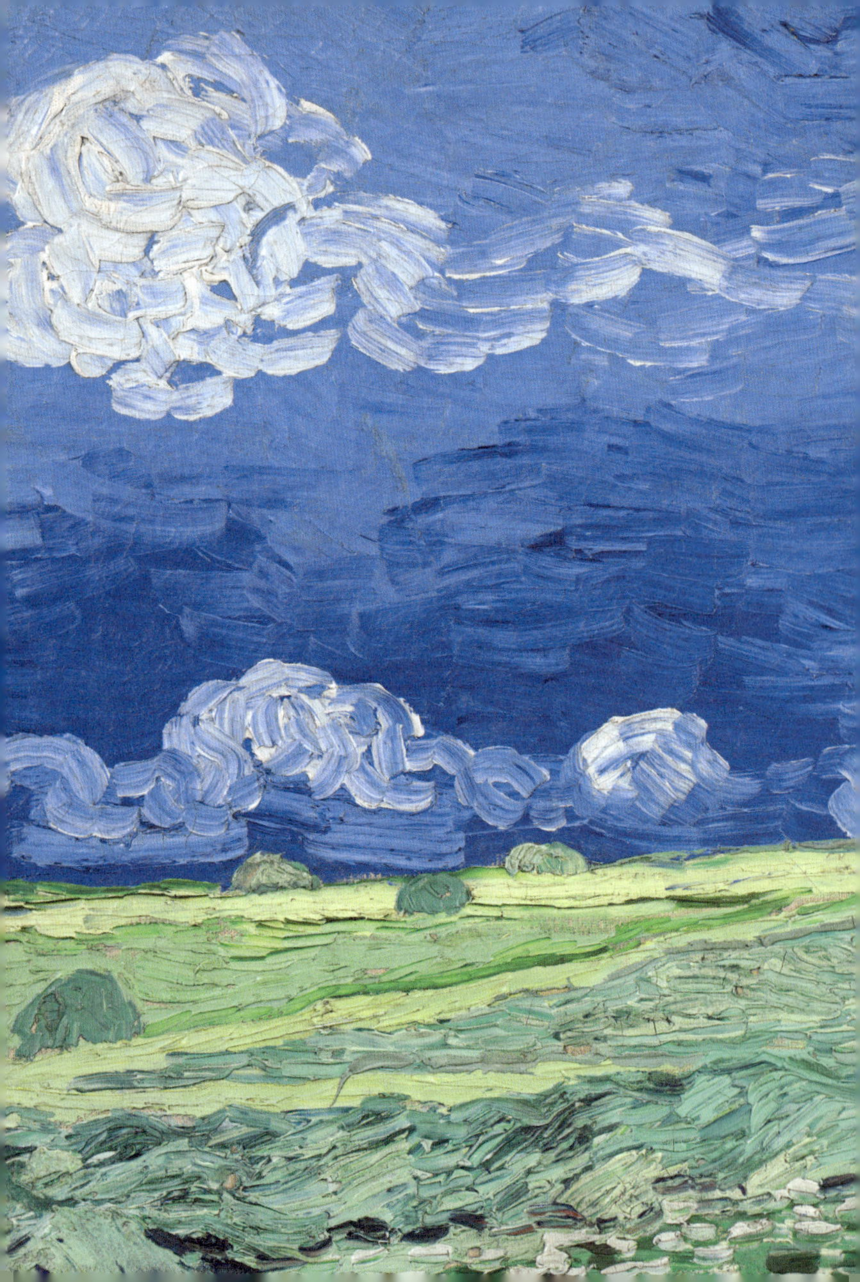

VAN GOGH ON ART

I'm an artist – which I won't take back, because those words naturally imply always seeking without ever fully finding.

Ideas for work are coming to me *in abundance*, and that means that even though isolated I don't have time to think or to feel. I'm going like a painting-locomotive.

~

I believe that certainly it's better to bring up children than to expend all one's nervous energy in making paintings [...]

~

Rembrandt goes so deep into the mysterious that he says things for which there are no words in any language.

~

You see what I've found, my work, and you also see what I haven't found, everything else that's part of life.

So then my brush goes between my fingers as if it were a bow on the violin and absolutely for my pleasure.

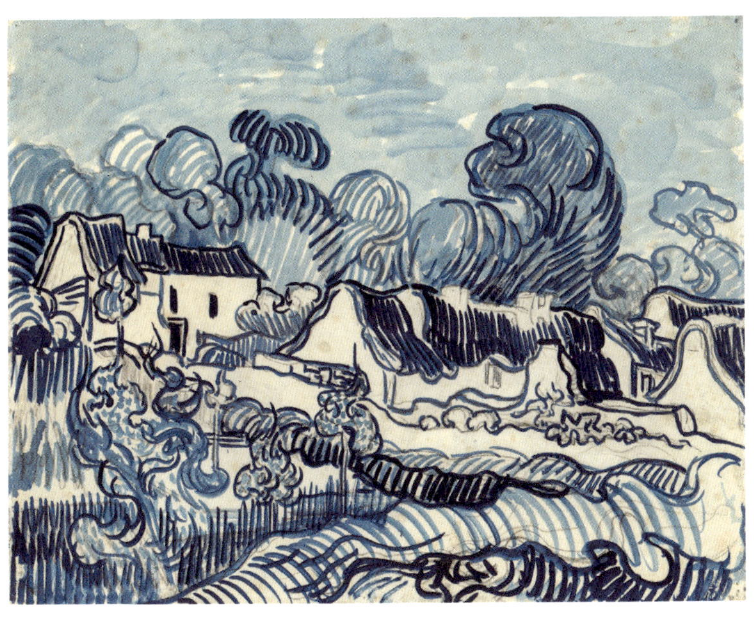

Landscape with Houses, 1890, pencil, brush and oil paint and watercolour on paper, 44 × 54.4 cm (17⅜ × 21½ in.)

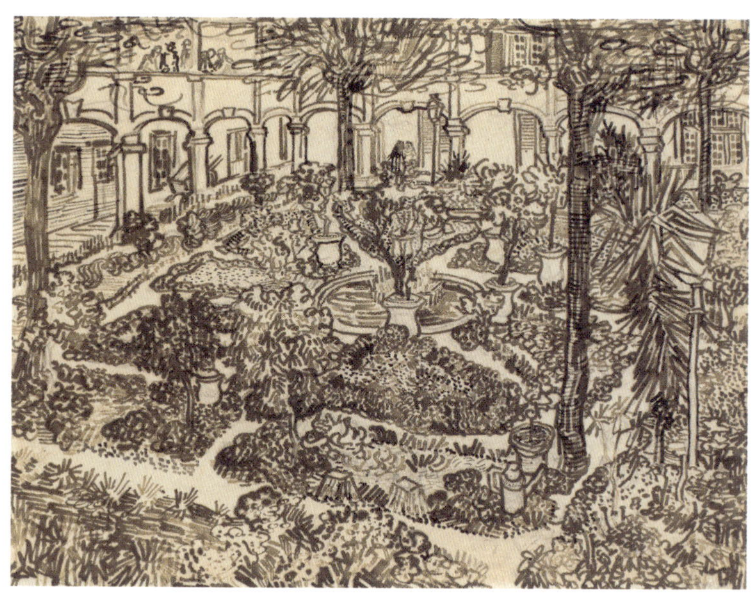

Garden of the Hospital, 1889, pencil, reed pen and pen and brush and ink on paper, 46.6 × 59.9 cm (18⅜ × 23⅝ in.)

I believe that at present we must paint nature's rich and magnificent aspects; we need good cheer and happiness, hope and love.

I'd rather paint people's eyes than cathedrals, for there's something in the eyes that isn't in the cathedral – although it's solemn and although it's impressive – to my mind the soul of a person [...] is more interesting.

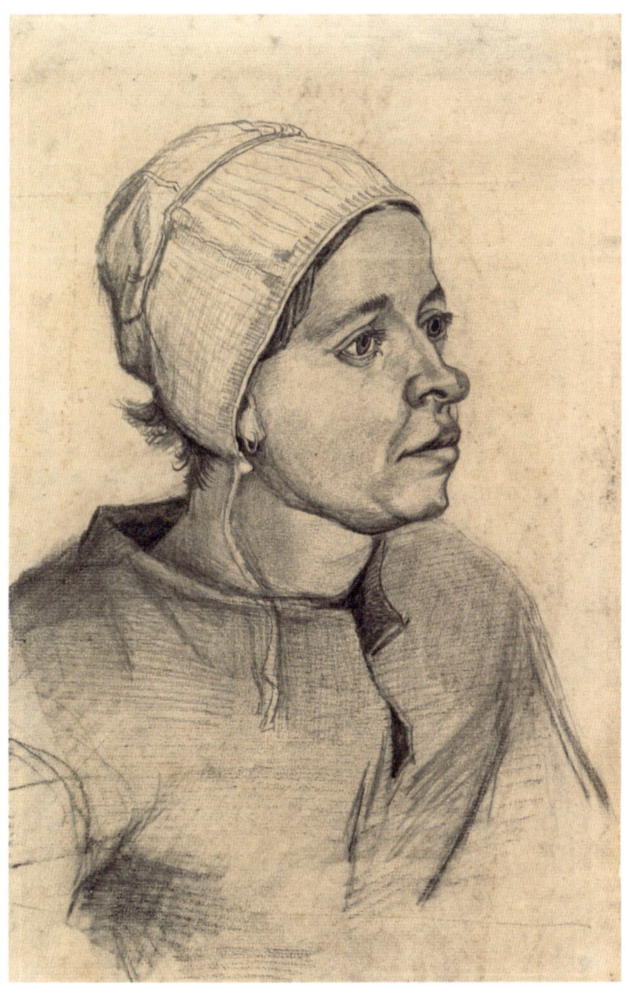

Head of a Woman, 1884–85, pencil and chalk on paper, 33.6 × 20 cm (13¼ × 7⅞ in.)

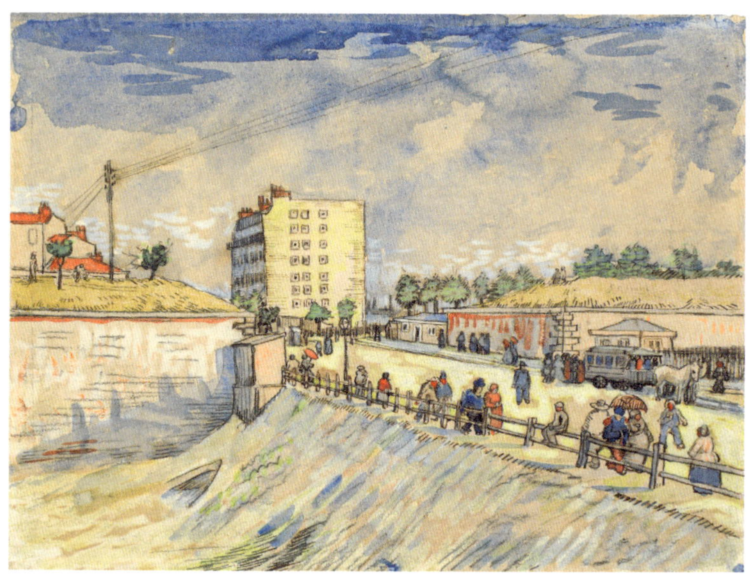

Gate in the Paris Ramparts, 1887, pencil, pen and ink, watercolour on paper, 24.1 × 31.6 cm (9½ × 12½ in.)

Almost no one knows that the secret of beautiful work is to a large extent good faith and sincere feeling.

How much there
is in art that is
beautiful, if only
one can remember
what one has seen,
one is never empty
or truly lonely,
and never alone.

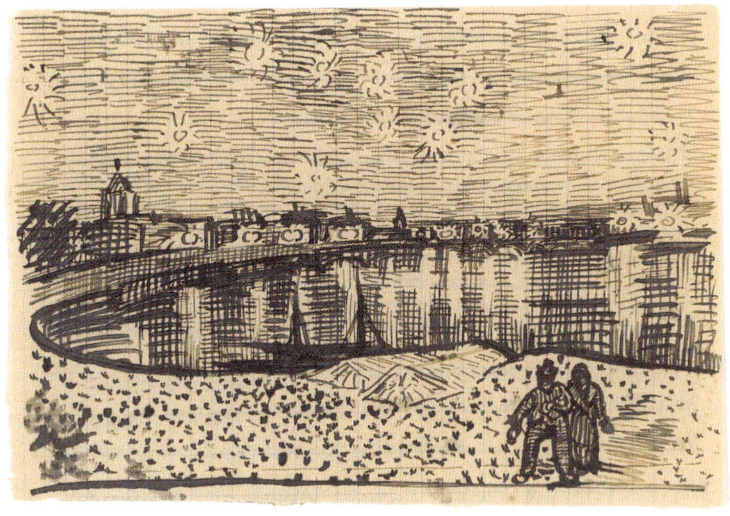

Sketch of *Starry Night Over the Rhône*, enclosed in a letter to Eugène Boch, Arles, 2 October 1888, pen and ink on paper, 9.5 × 13.5 cm (3¾ × 5⅜ in.)

It *is no easier*, I'm convinced, to make a good painting than to find a diamond or a pearl.

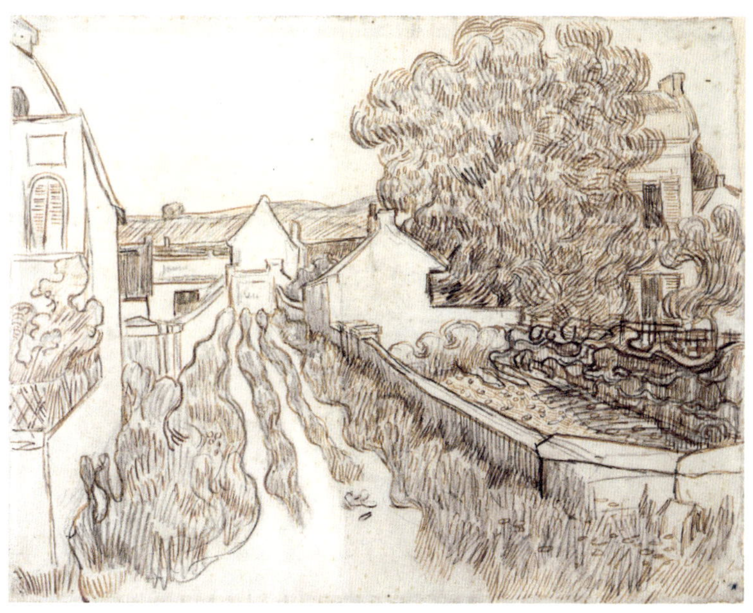

Dead-End Street with Houses, 1890, pencil, pen and ink on paper, 45 × 55.6 cm (17¾ × 22 in.)

You don't know how *paralyzing* it is, that *stare* from a blank canvas that says to the painter *you can't do anything*. [...] Many painters *are afraid* of the blank *canvas*, but the blank canvas is AFRAID of the truly passionate painter who dares.

~

There are so many people [...] who imagine that words are nothing. On the contrary, don't you think, it's as interesting and as difficult to say a thing well as to paint a thing. There's the art of lines and colours, but there's the art of words that will last just the same.

Art is jealous
and demands
all our time,
all our strength.

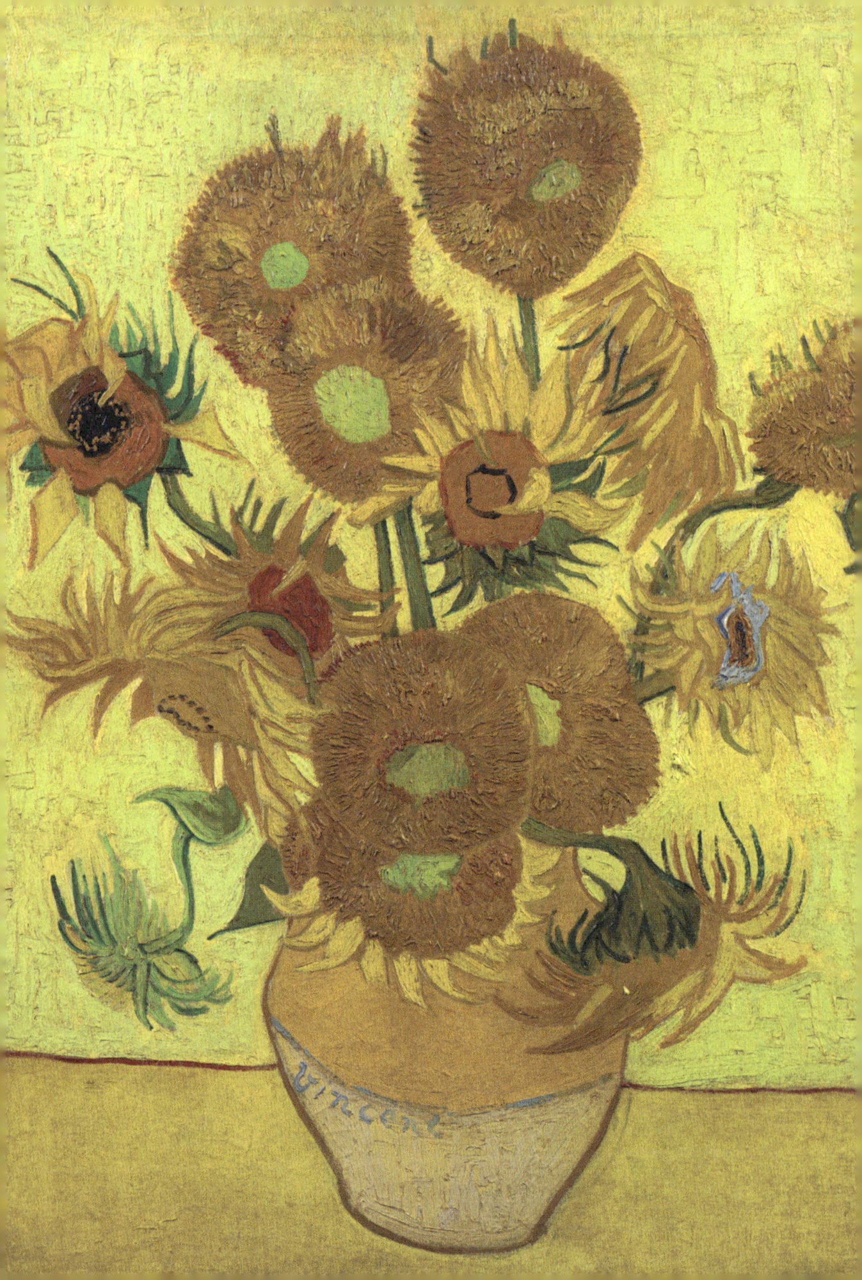
Vincent

VAN GOGH
ON COLOUR

The uglier, older, meaner, iller, poorer I get, the more I wish to take my revenge by doing brilliant colour, well arranged, resplendent.

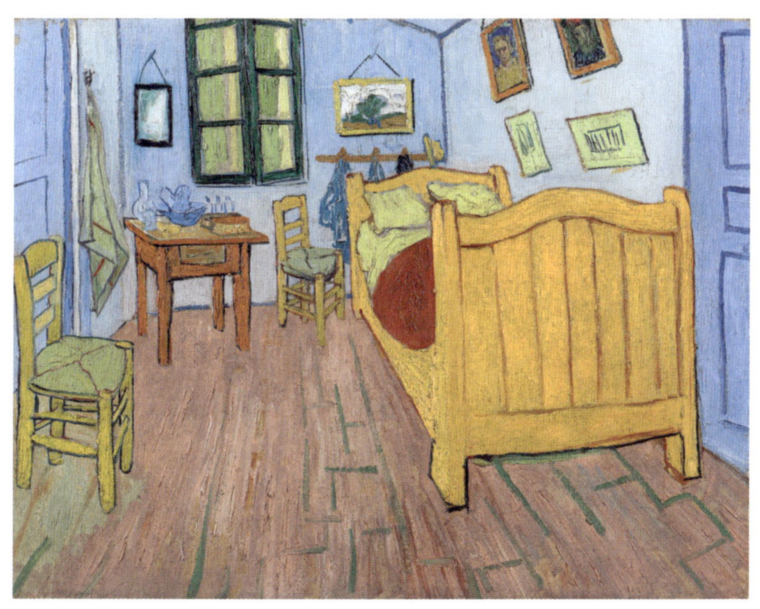

The Bedroom, 1888, oil on canvas, 72.4 × 91.3 cm (28⅝ × 36 in.)

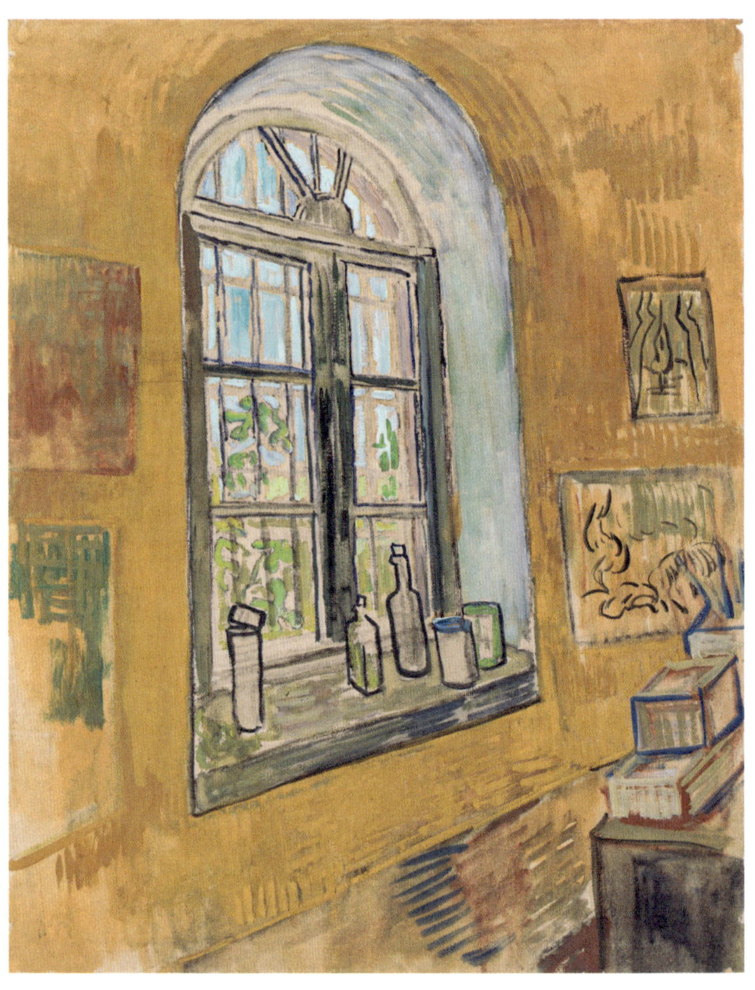

Window in the Studio, 1889, chalk, brush and oil paint and watercolour on paper, 62 × 47.6 cm (24½ × 18¾ in.)

What a great thing tone and colour are! And anyone who doesn't acquire a feeling for it, how far removed from life he will remain!

COLOUR EXPRESSES SOMETHING IN ITSELF. One can't do without it; one must make use of it. What looks beautiful, really beautiful – is also right.

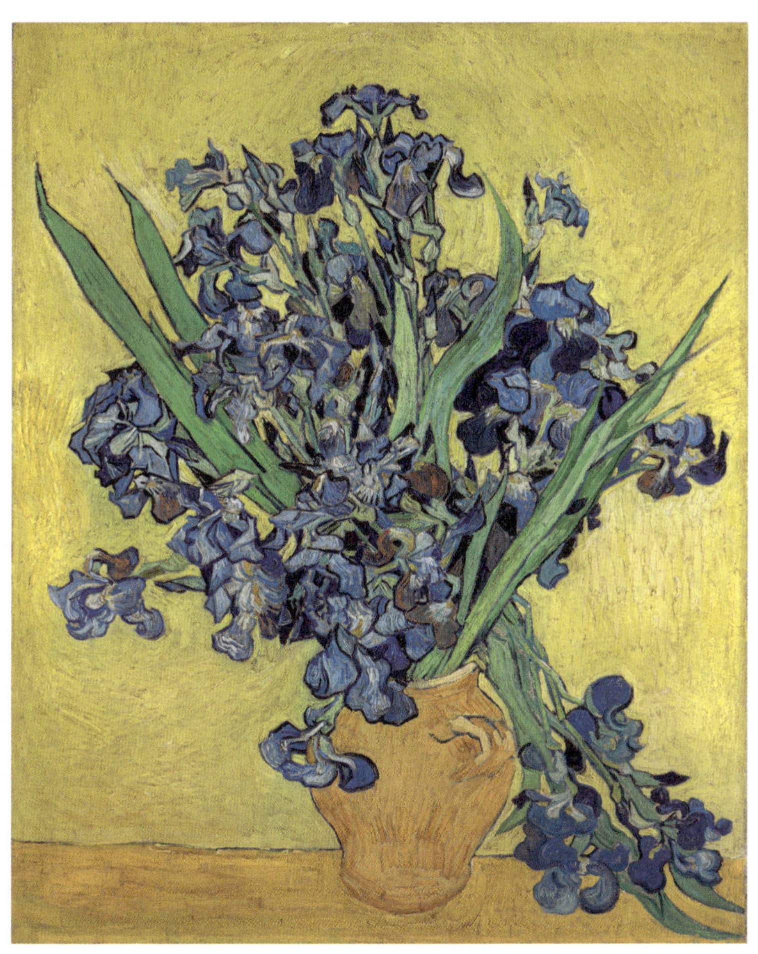

Irises, 1890, oil on canvas, 92.7 × 73.9 cm (36½ × 29⅛ in.)

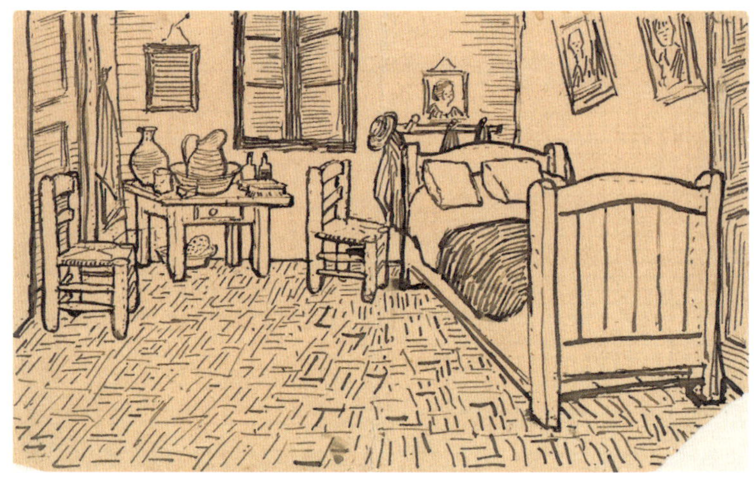

Sketch of *The Bedroom*, enclosed in a letter to Theo, Arles, 16 October 1888, pen and ink on paper, 13 × 21 cm (5⅛ × 29⅛ in.)

But the painter
of the future is a
*colourist such as there
hasn't been before.*

It often seems to me that the night is much more alive and richly coloured than the day.

Because instead of trying to render exactly what I have before my eyes, I use colour more arbitrarily in order to express myself forcefully.

~

Arranging colours in a painting to make them shimmer and stand out through their contrasts, that's something like arranging jewels or – designing costumes.

~

What I'm most passionate about, much much more than all the rest in my profession – is the portrait, the modern portrait. I seek it by way of colour [...]

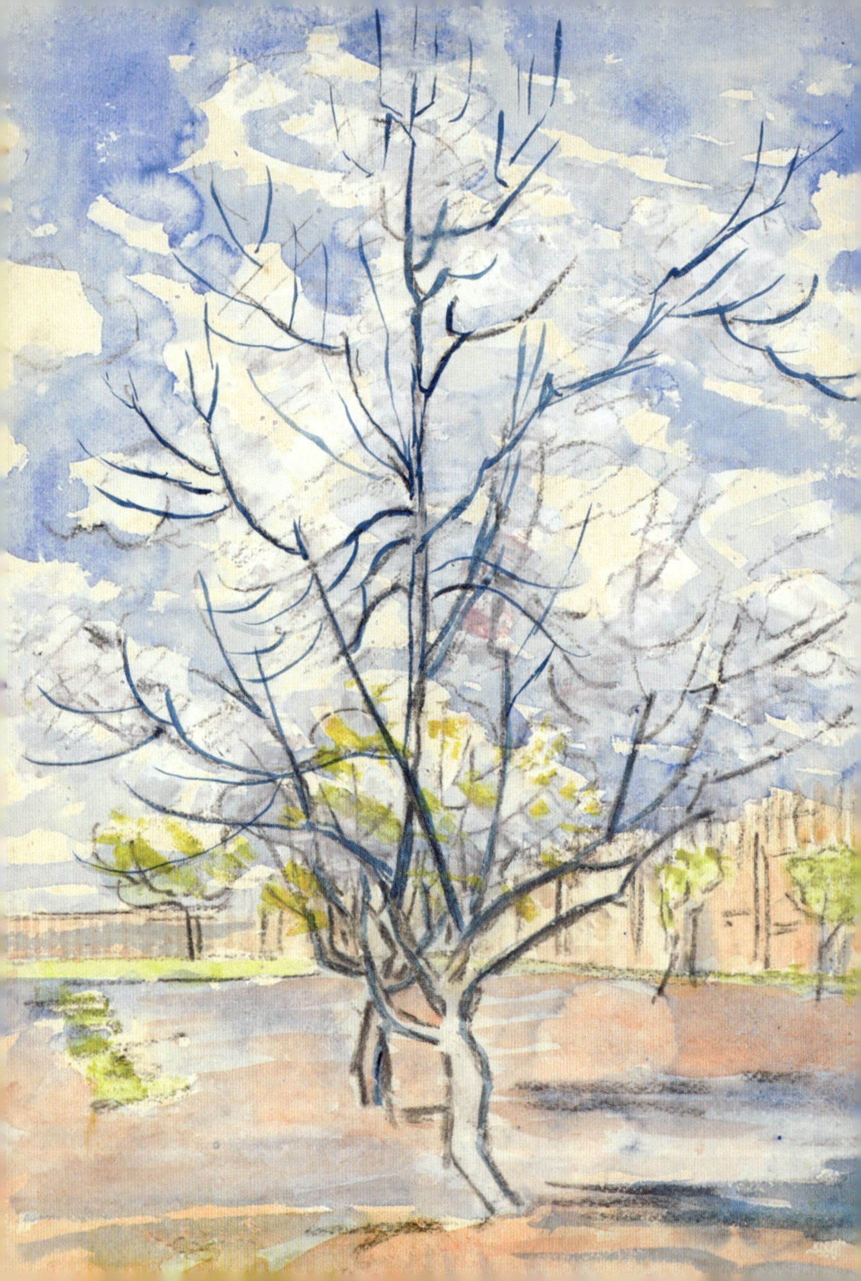

VAN GOGH ON NATURE

I have a terrible clarity of mind at times, when nature is so lovely these days, and then I'm no longer aware of myself and the painting comes to me as if in a dream.

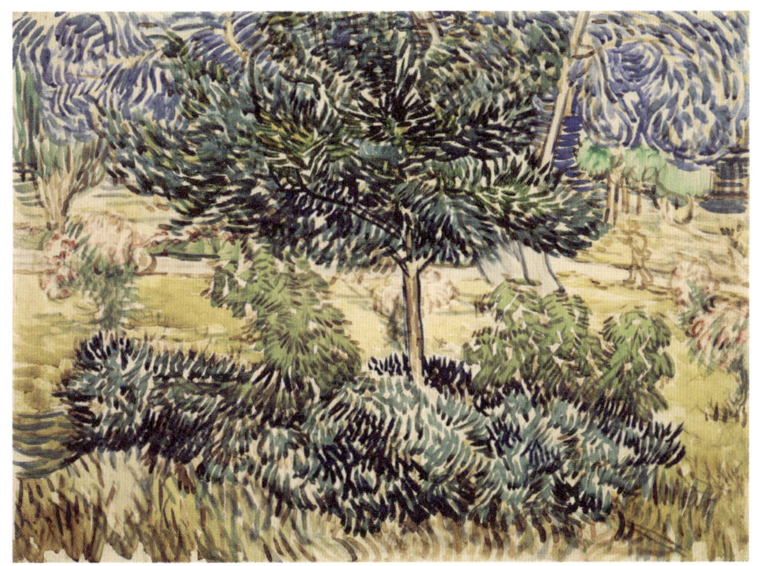

Tree and Bushes in the Garden of the Asylum, 1889, chalk, brush and oil paint and ink on paper, 46.9 × 61.9 cm (18½ × 24⅜ in.)

If one truly loves nature one finds beauty everywhere.

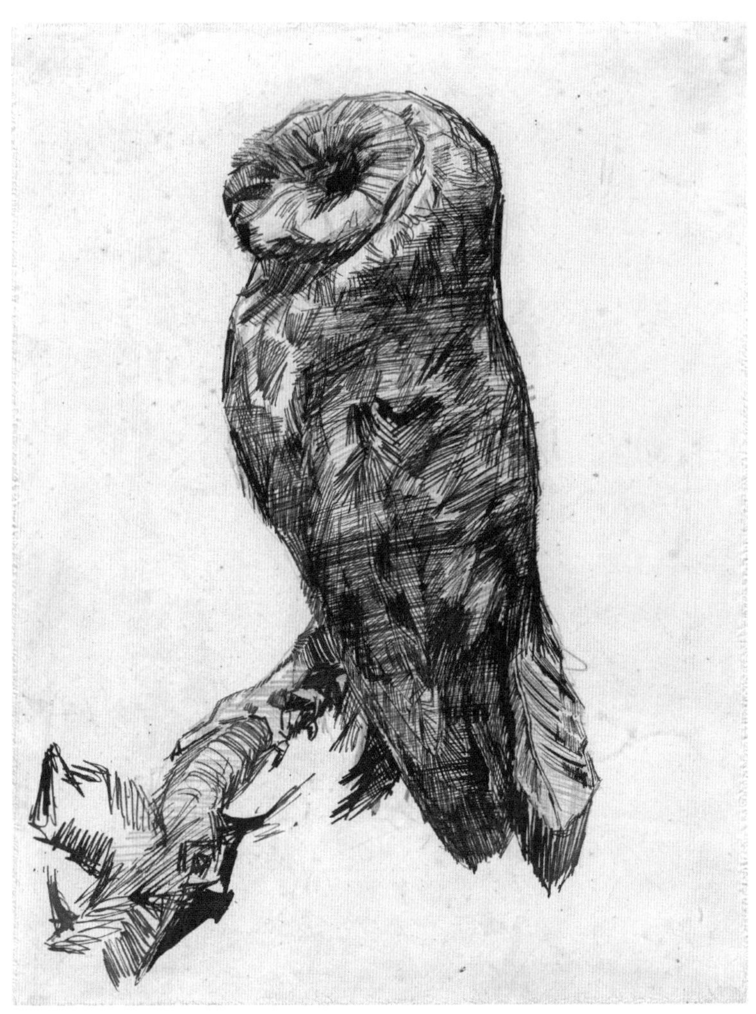

Barn Owl Viewed from the Side, 1887, pencil, pen and ink on paper, 35.3 × 26.2 cm (14 × 10⅜ in.)

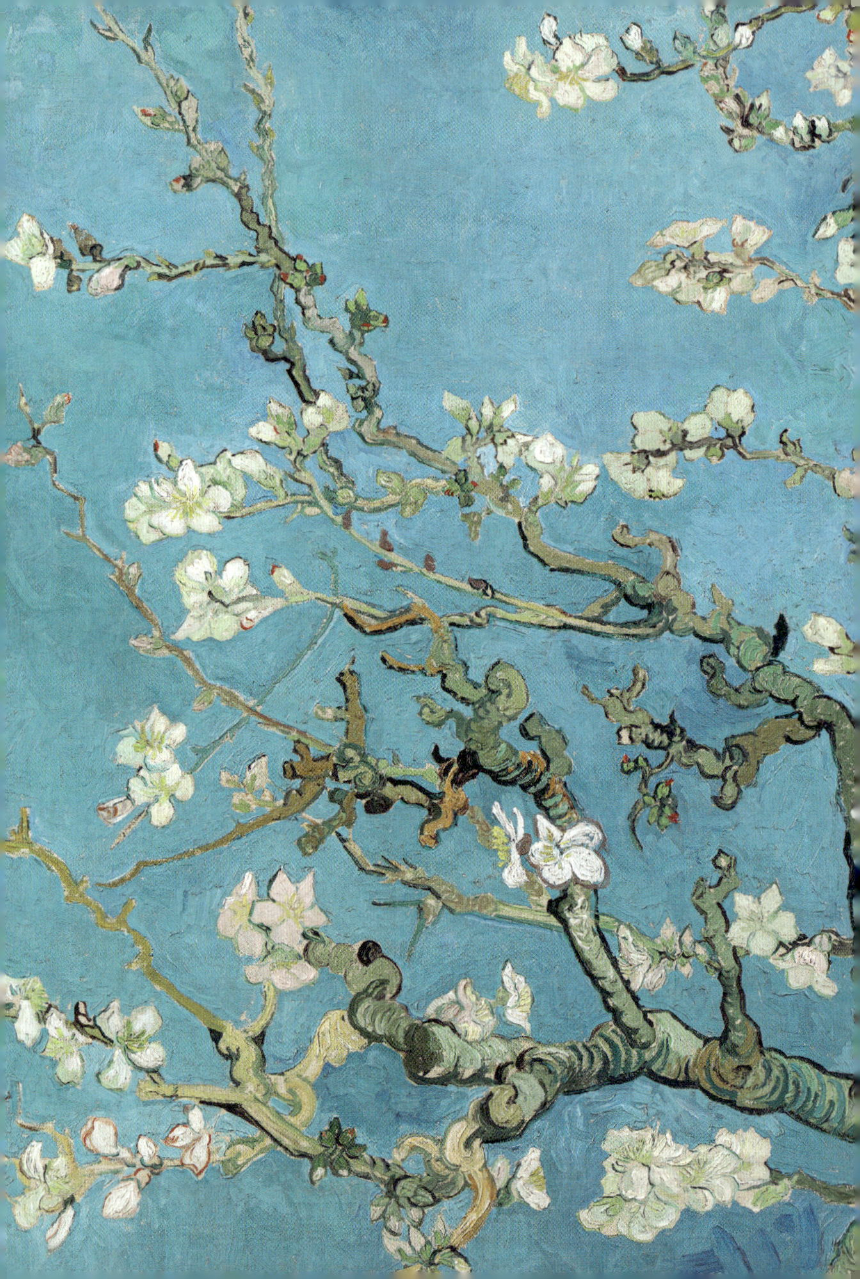

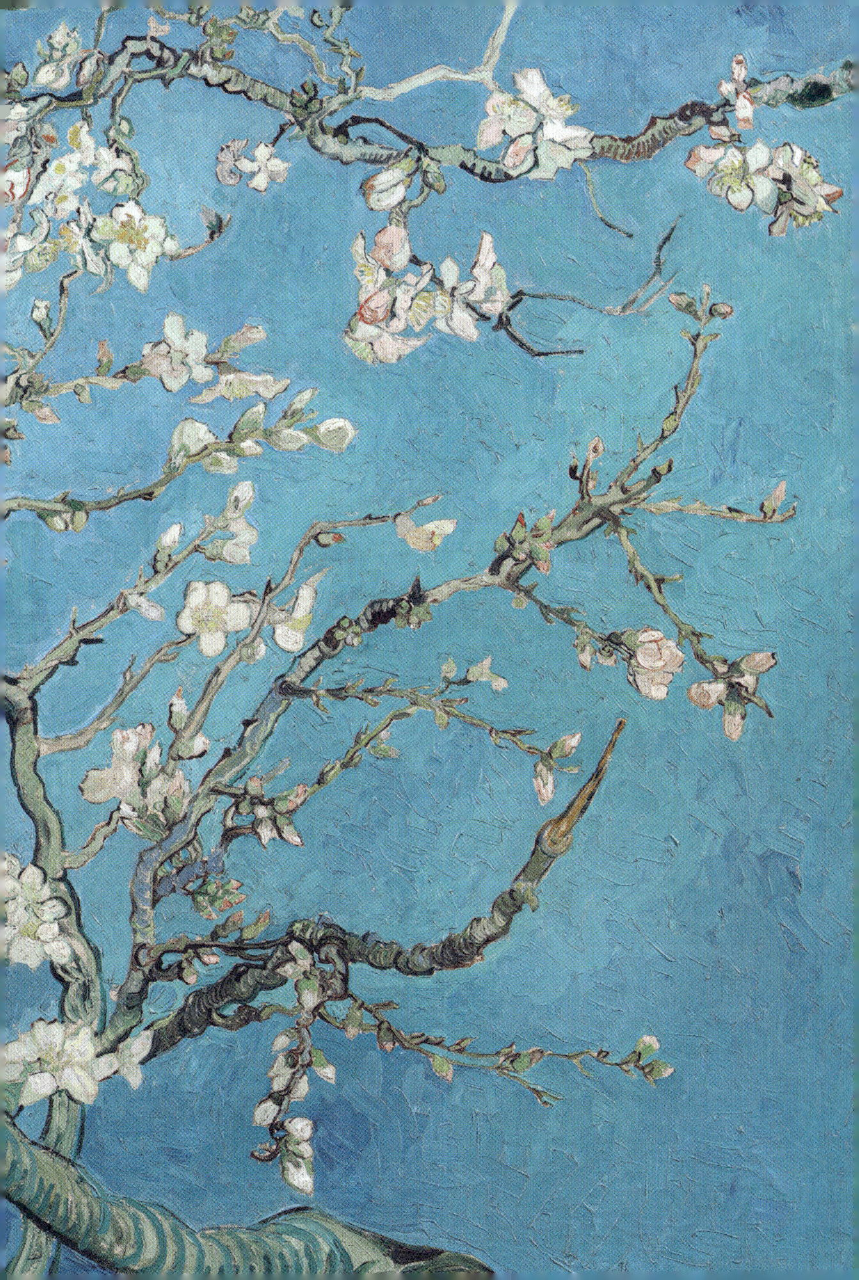

It isn’t the language of painters one ought to listen to but the language of nature.

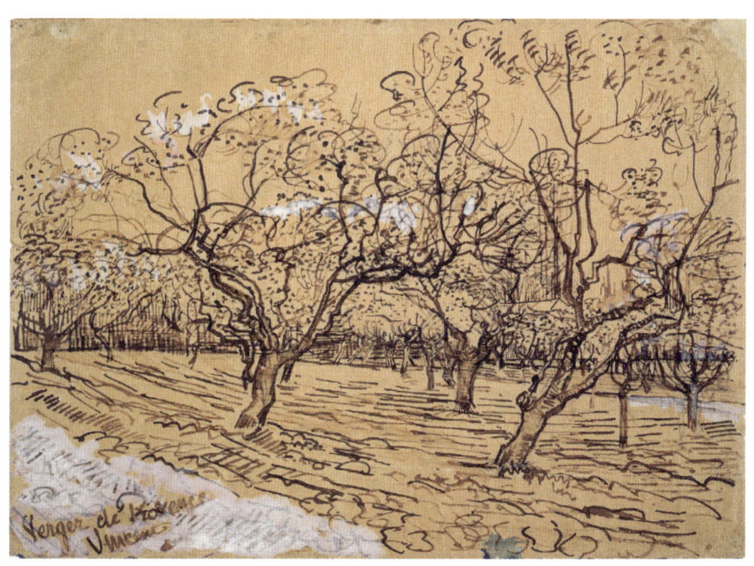

Provençal Orchard, 1888, pencil, pen and reed pen and ink, watercolour on paper, 39.4 × 53.6 cm (15⅝ × 21⅛ in.)

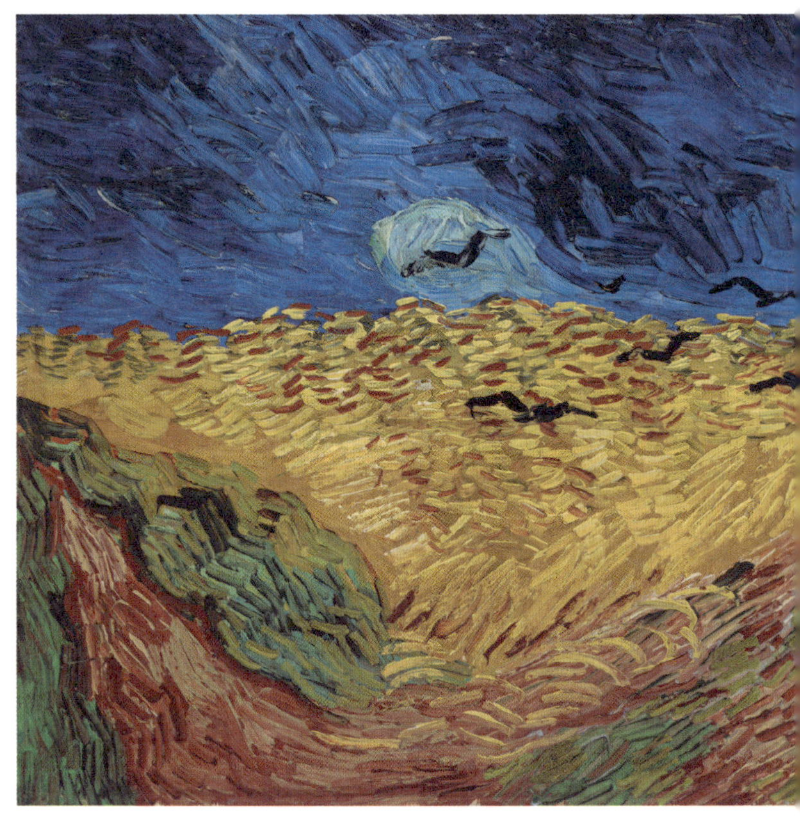

Wheatfield with Crows, 1890, oil on canvas, 50.5 × 103 cm (20 × 40⅝ in.)

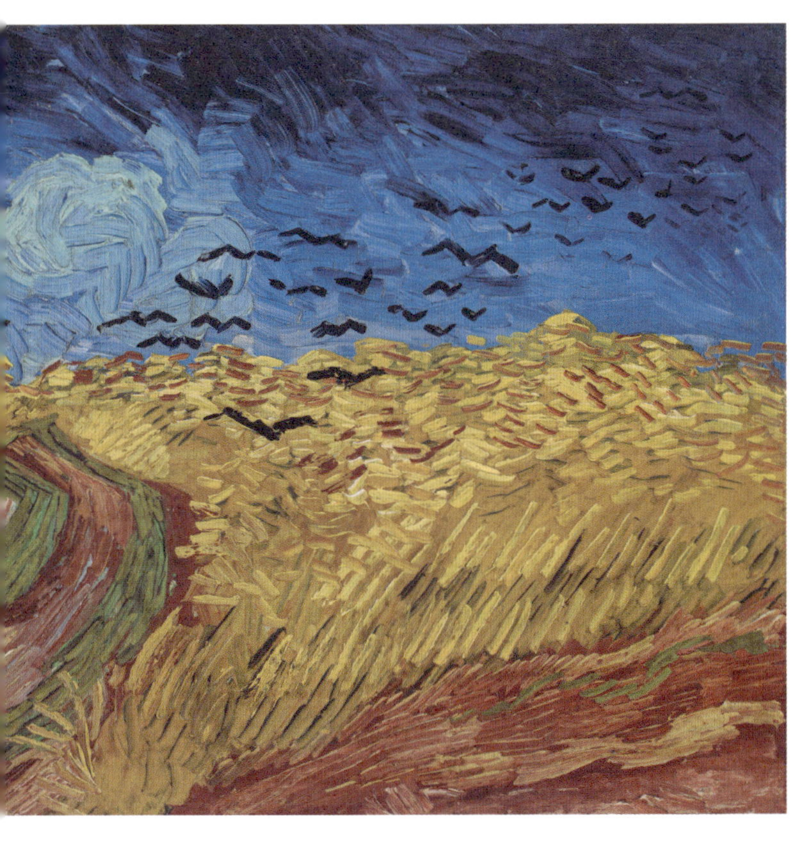

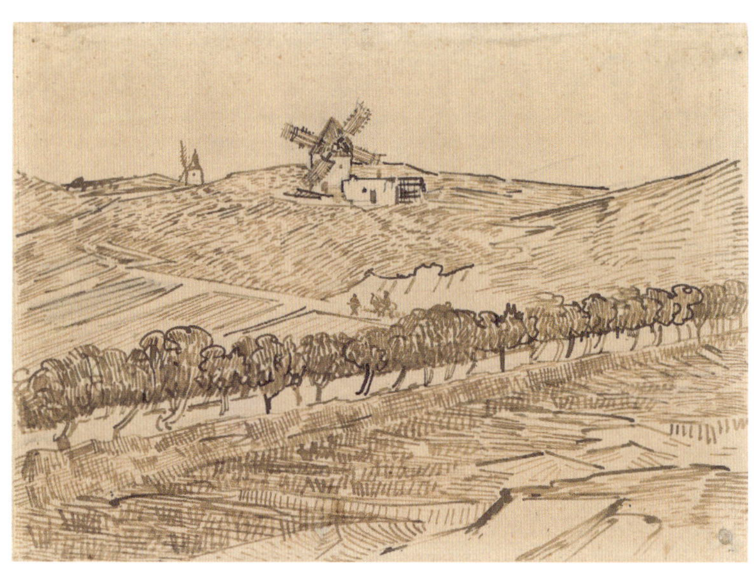

Landscape with Windmills at Fontvieille, 1888, pencil, pen and reed pen and ink on paper, 25.8 × 34.7 cm (10¼ × 13¾ in.)

In my life as a painter, and above all when I'm in the country, it's not so difficult for me to be alone, because in the country one feels the bonds that unite us all more easily.

What we need is sunshine and fine weather and blue air as the most dependable remedy.

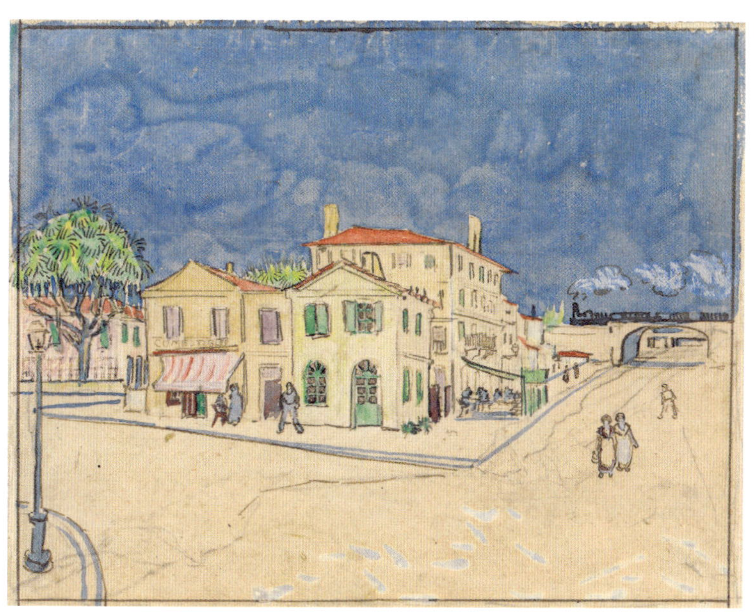

The Yellow House (The Street), 1888, pencil, reed pen and pen and ink, watercolour on paper, 25.7 × 32 cm (10⅛ × 12⅝ in.)

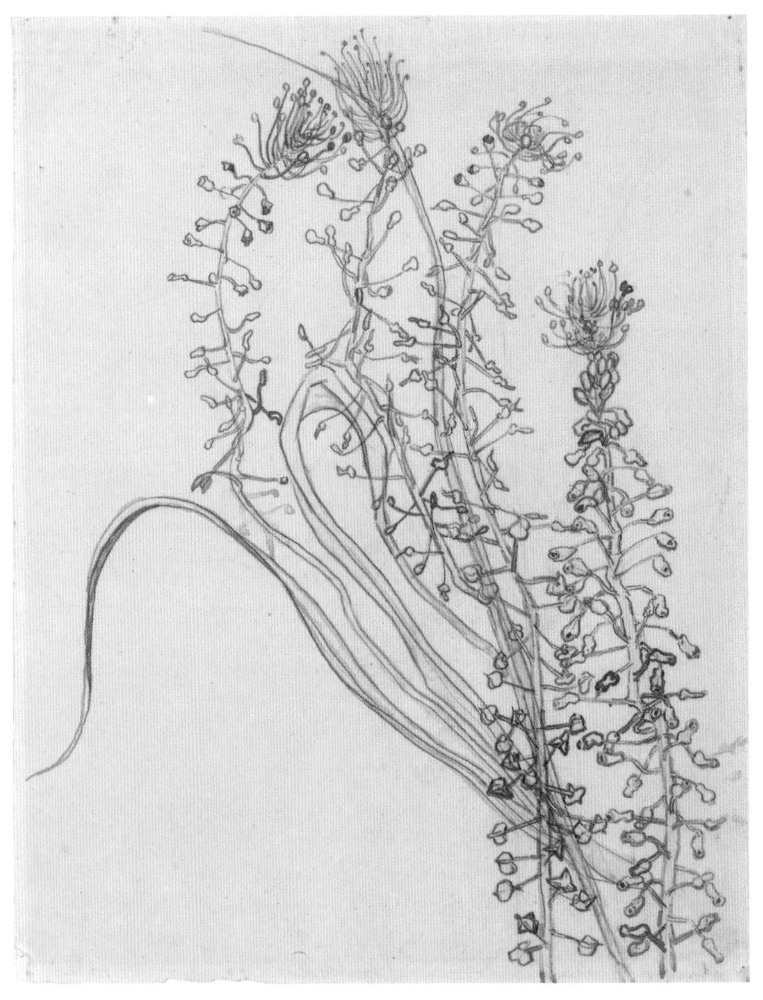

Tassel Hyacinth, 1889, pencil, brush and ink on paper, 41.2 × 30.9 cm (12⅜ × 12¼ in.)

I see in my work
an echo of what
struck me, I see
that nature has
told me something,
has spoken to
me and that I've
written it down
in shorthand.

Always continue walking a lot and loving nature, for that's the real way to learn to understand art better and better.

How much good it does a person if one is in a gloomy mood to walk on the empty beach and look into the grey-green sea with the long white lines of the waves.

~

Do you get up early? I do regularly, it's good to make a habit of it. It's precious and already very dear to me, that early morning twilight.

~

Sometimes I long so much to do landscape, just as one would for a long walk to refresh oneself, and in all of nature, in trees for instance, I see expression and a soul, as it were. A row of pollard willows sometimes resembles a procession of orphan men.

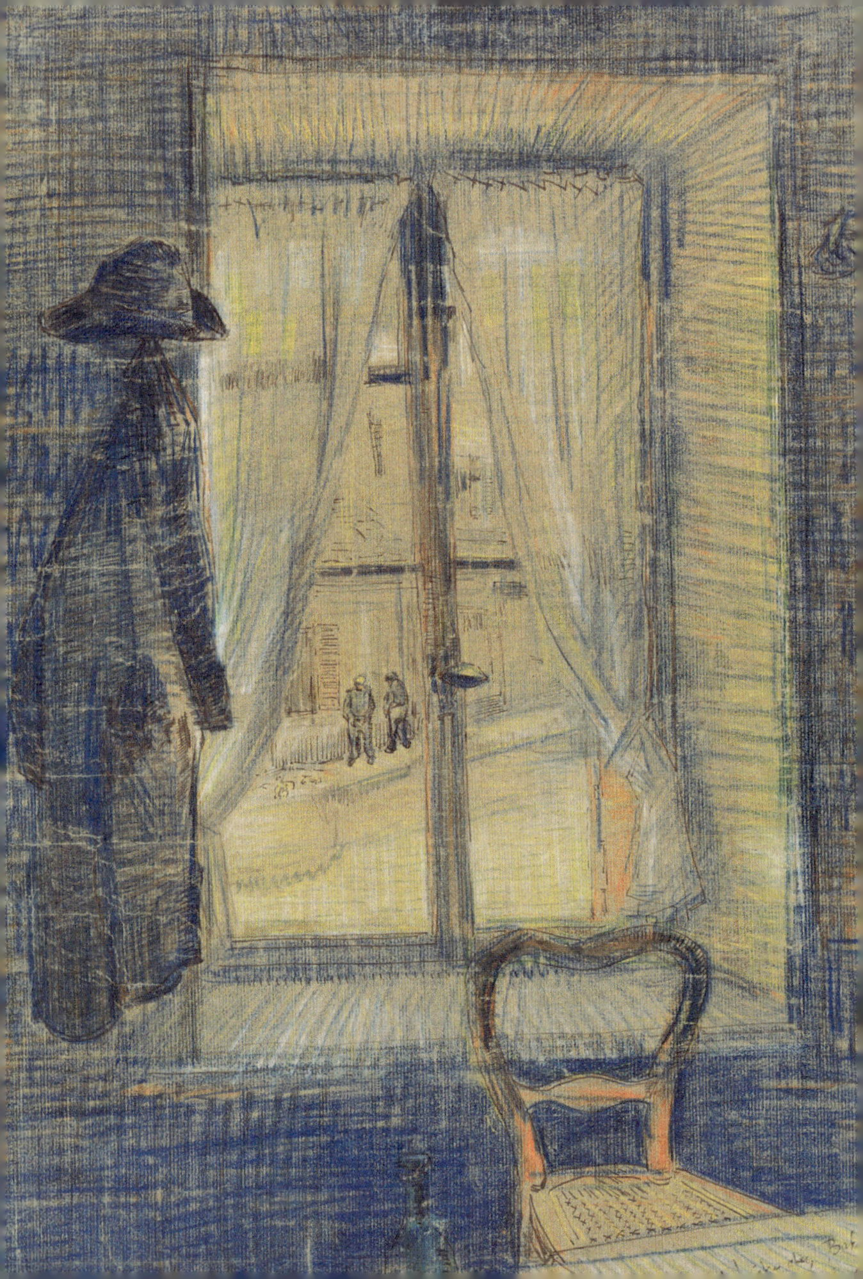

VAN GOGH ON AMBITION

I feel a power in me
that I must develop,
a fire that I may
not put out but
must fan, although
I don't know to
what outcome
it will lead me.

I have a more or less irresistible passion for books, and I have a need continually to educate myself, to study, if you like, precisely as I need to eat my bread.

~

I know too well what aim I have in view, I'm too absolutely and utterly convinced that I am, after all, on the right path – when I want to paint what I feel and feel what I paint – to worry too much about what people say of me.

~

The more I become dissipated, ill, a broken pitcher, the more I too become a creative artist in that great revival of art of which we're speaking.

~

What I want and set as my goal is damned difficult, and yet I don't believe I'm aiming too high.

And in a painting
I'd like to say
something
consoling, like
a piece of music.

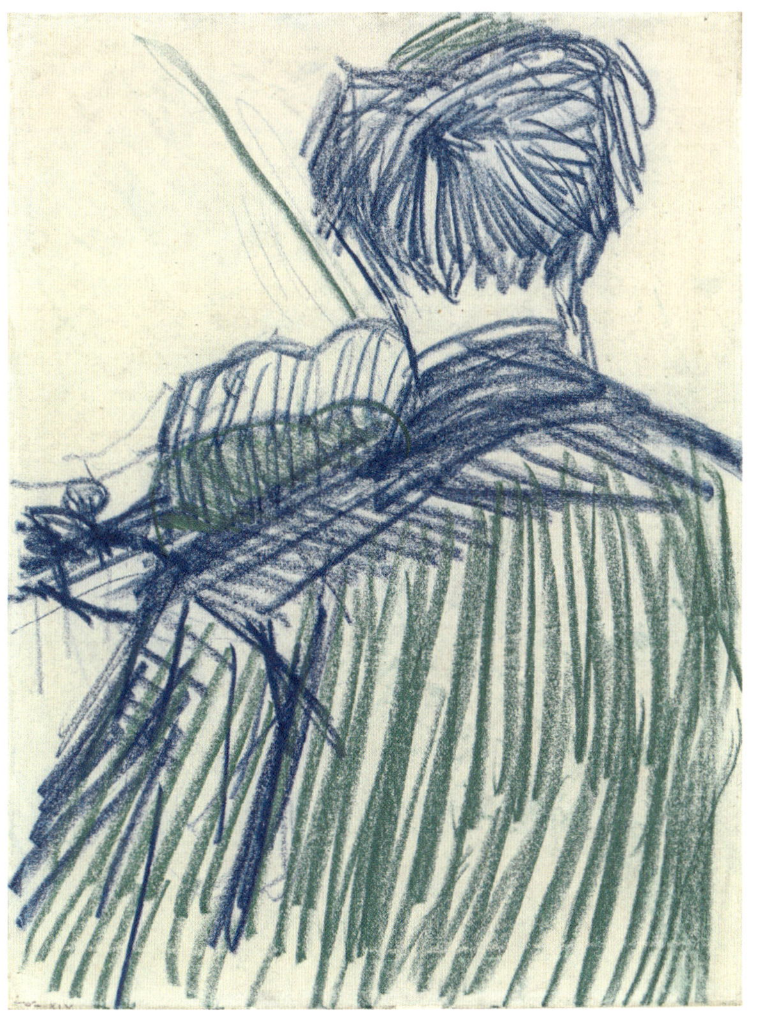

Violinist Seen from the Back, 1887, chalk on paper, 34.9 × 25.8 cm (13¾ × 10¼ in.)

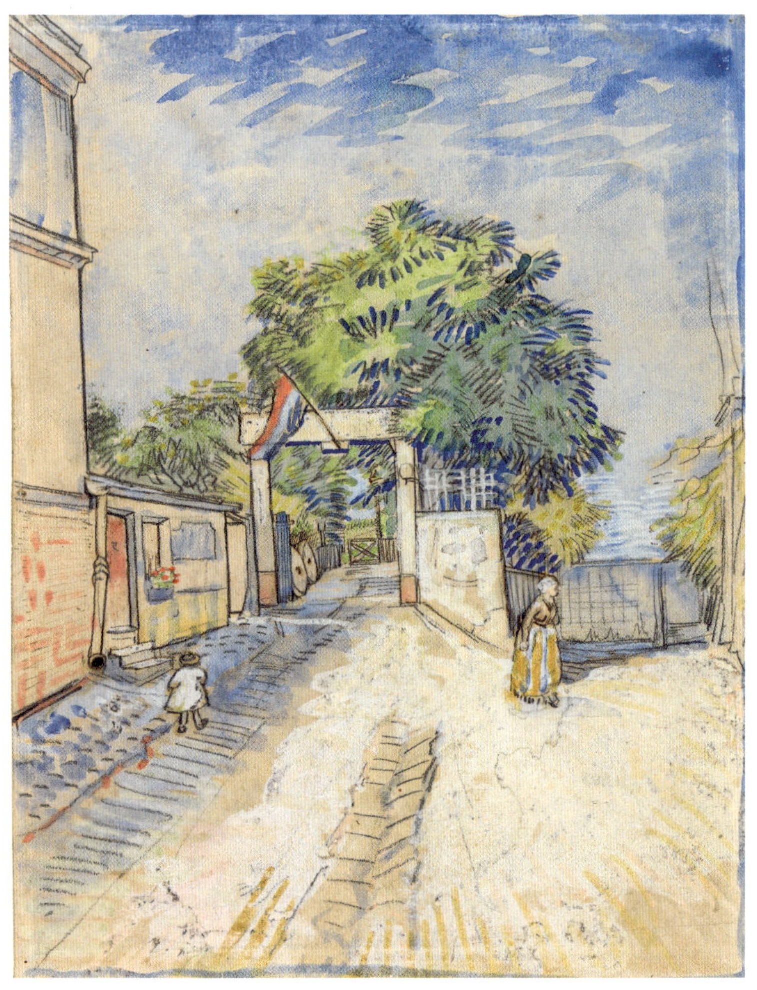

Entrance to the Moulin de la Galette, 1887, pencil, pen and ink, watercolour on paper, 31.6 × 24 cm (12½ × 9½ in.)

The creative power can't be held back, what one feels must come out.

I want to make drawings that *move* some people. [...] I want to reach the point where people say of my work, that man feels deeply and that man feels subtly.

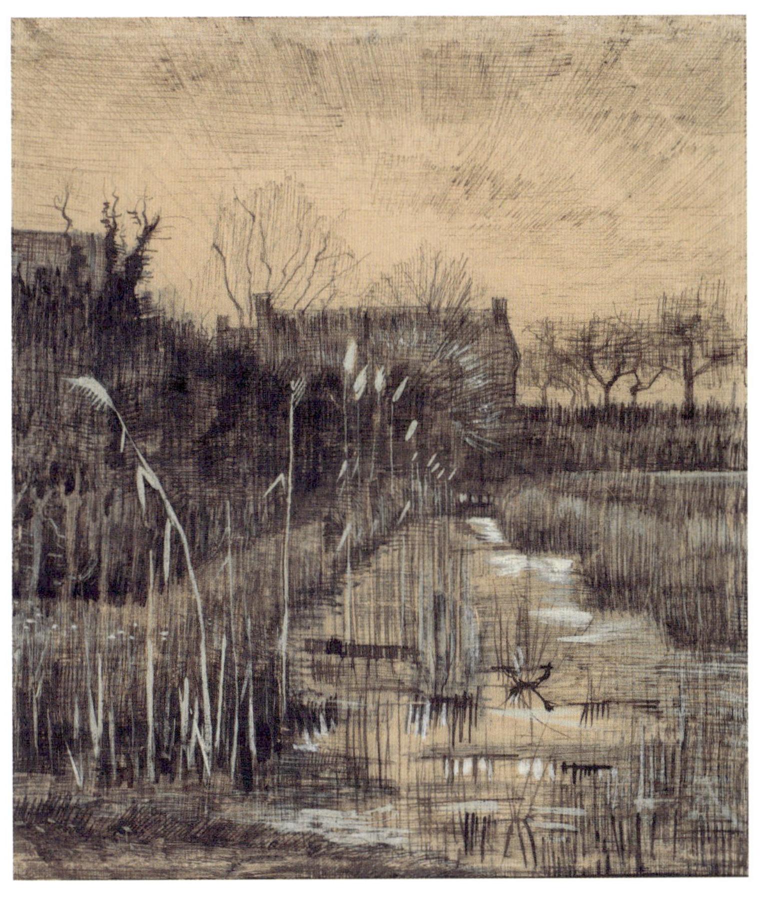

Ditch, 1884, pencil, pen and ink, paint on paper, 42.3 × 34.5 cm (16¾ × 14 in.)

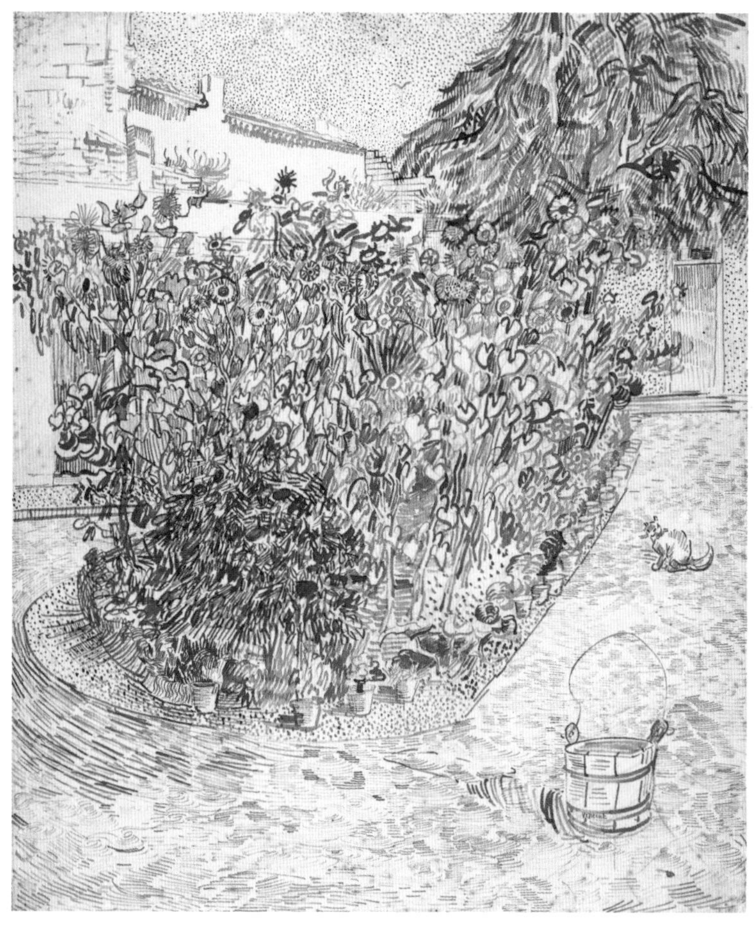

Garden of a Bathhouse, 1888, pencil, reed pen and brush and ink on paper, 60.7 × 49.2 cm (24 × 19⅜ in.)

Look, a canvas
that I cover is
worth more than
a blank canvas.

It's a wonderful thing to look at something and find it beautiful, to reflect on it and hold it fast and then to say: I'm going to draw that, and then to work on it until it's done.

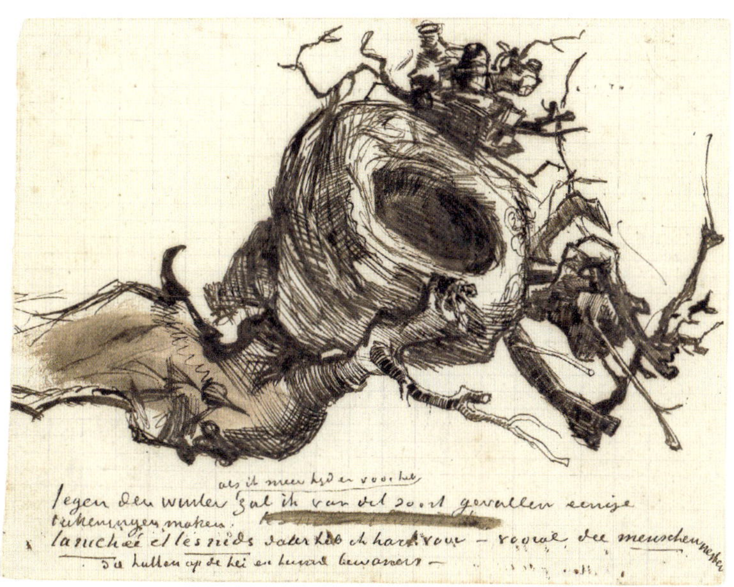

Letter to Theo with sketch of *Bird's Nest*, Nuenen, 4 October 1885, pen and ink on paper, 11 × 16.8 cm (4⅜ × 6⅝ in.)

I keep on making
what I can't do yet
in order to learn
to be able to do it.

I feel that my work lies in the heart of the people, that I must keep close to the ground, that I must delve deeply into life and must get ahead by coping with great cares and difficulties.

~

Through working hard, old chap, I hope to make something good one day. I haven't got it yet, but I'm hunting it and fighting for it [...]

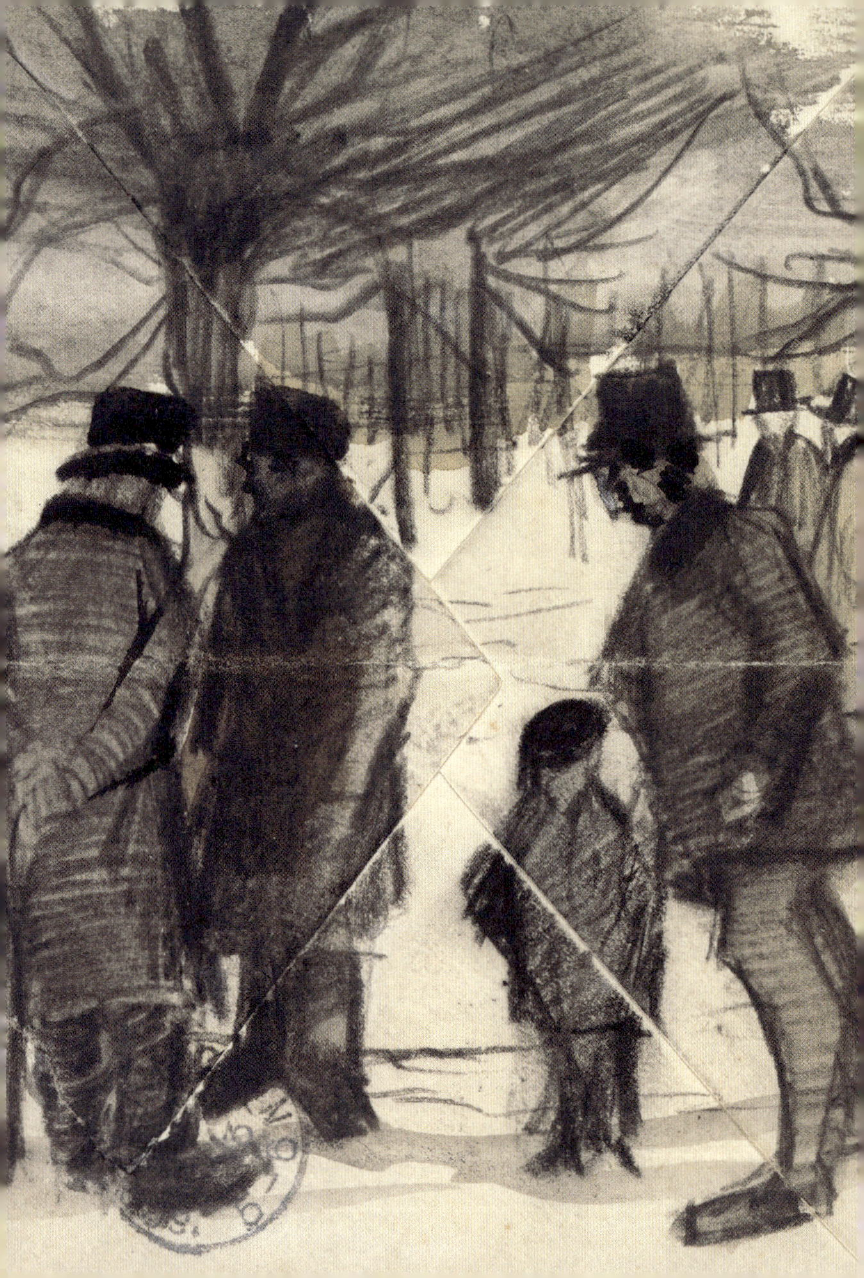

VAN GOGH
ON
CHARACTER

Don't imagine that I think myself perfect – or that I believe it isn't my fault that many people find me a disagreeable character.

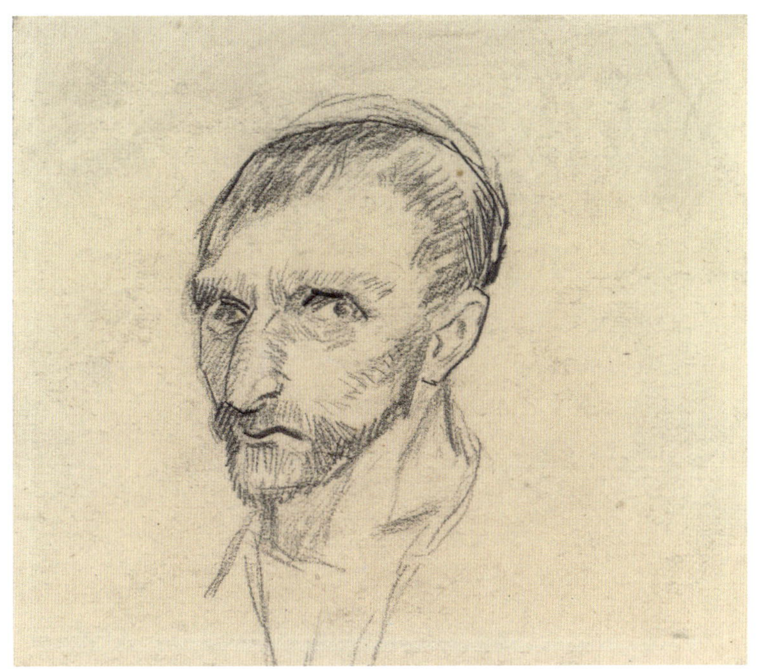

Self-Portrait, 1887, pencil on paper, 19.2 × 21.1 cm (7⅝ × 8⅜ in.)

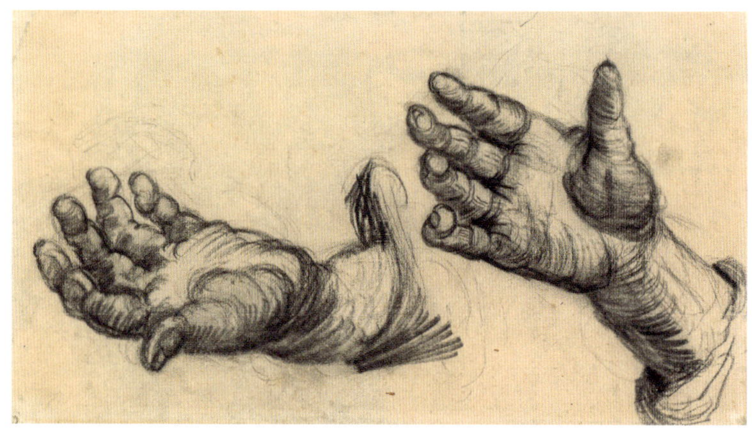

Two Hands, 1884–85, chalk on paper, 21.1 × 34.6 cm (8⅜ × 13⅝ in.)

I can't always sit quietly by; it sometimes seems to me as if people are physically touching me [...] so much is my conviction sometimes a part of myself.

I, for one, am a man of passions, capable of and liable to do rather foolish things for which I sometimes feel rather sorry.

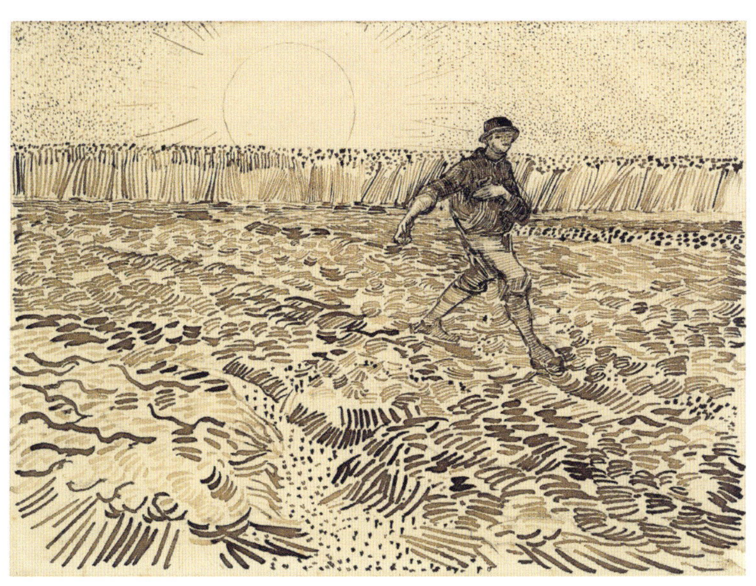

The Sower, 1888, pencil, pen and reed pen and ink on paper, 24.4 × 32 cm (9⅝ × 12⅝ in.)

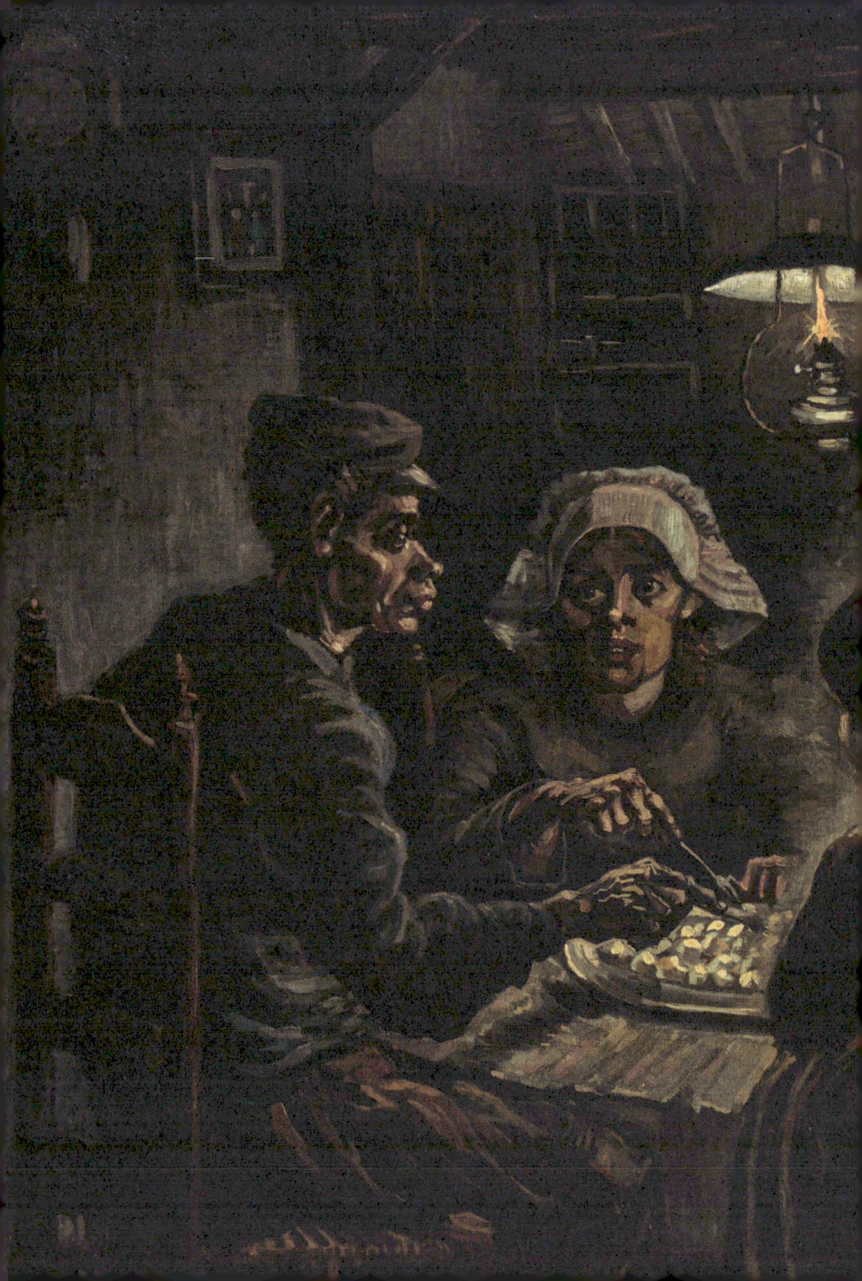

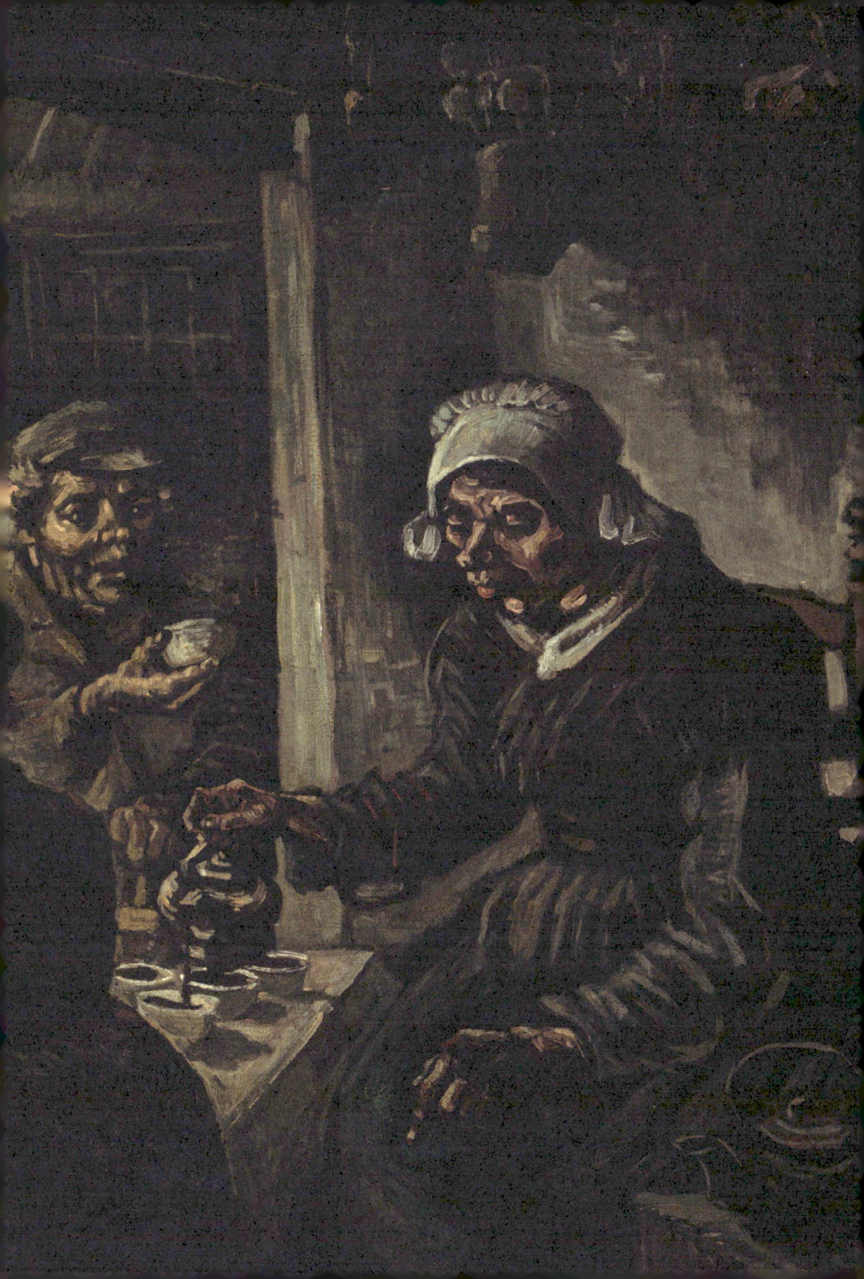

People say – and I'm quite willing to believe it – that it's difficult to know oneself – but it's not easy to paint oneself either.

I am not an adventurer by choice but by fate and feeling nowhere so much myself a stranger as in my family and country.

~

I think that if I didn't give vent to my feelings once in a while the boiler would burst.

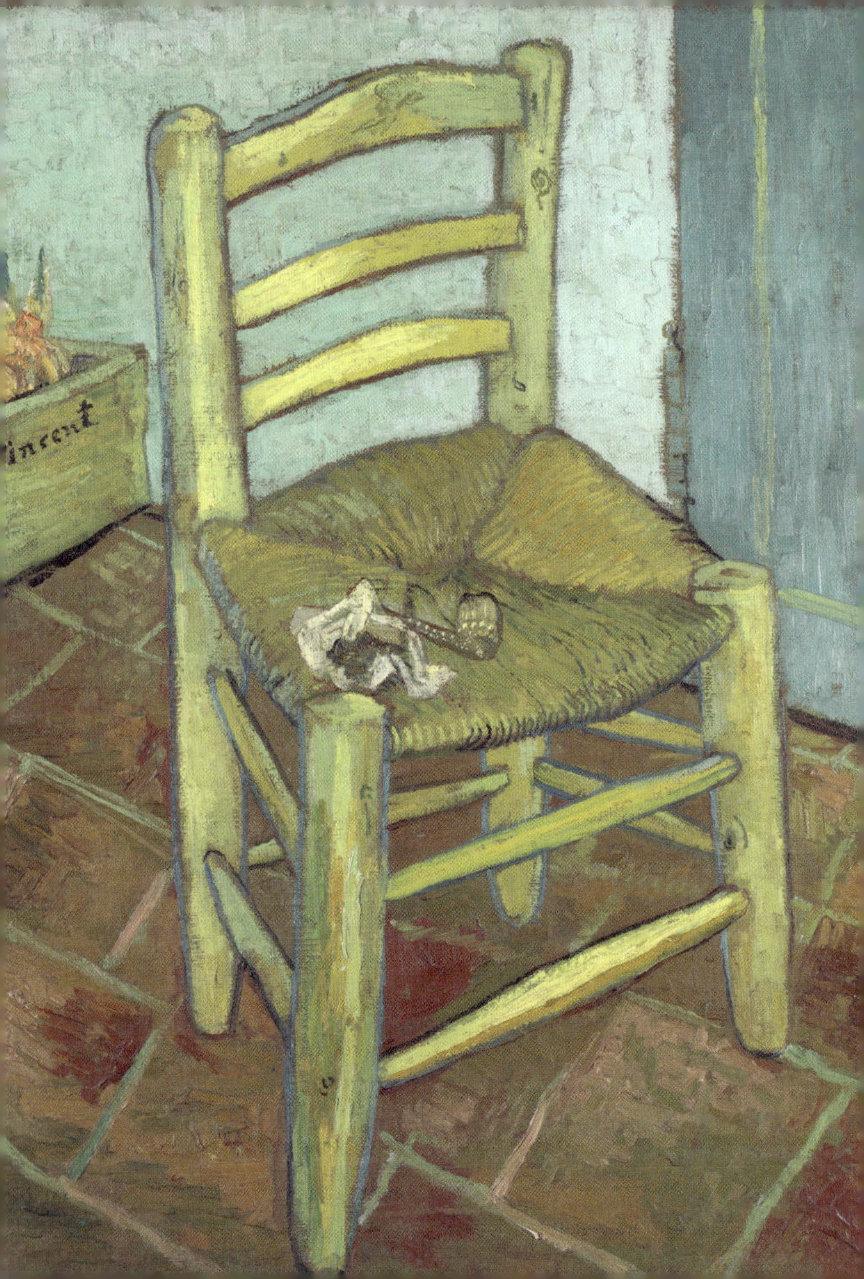
incent

VAN GOGH
ON ILLNESS

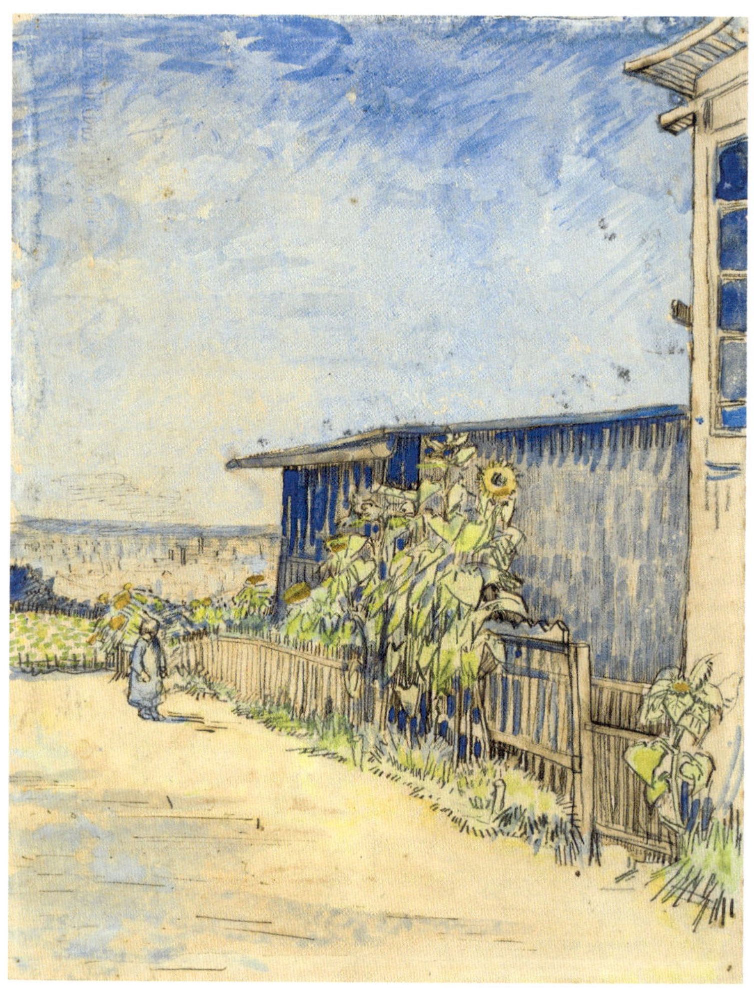

Shed with Sunflowers, 1887, pencil, pen and ink, watercolour on paper, 31.6 × 24.1 cm (12½ × 9½ in.)

Oh, the beautiful
sun down here in
high summer; it beats
down on your head
and I have no doubt
at all that it drives
you crazy. Now being
that way already,
all I do is enjoy it.

I'm struggling with
all my energy to
master my work,
telling myself
that if I win this
it will be the best
lightning conductor
for the illness.

I well knew that one could break one's arms and legs before, and that then afterwards that could get better but I didn't know that one could break one's brain and that afterwards that got better too.

~

We're all mortal and subject to all possible illnesses, what can we do about it when the latter aren't precisely of a pleasant kind. The best thing is to try to recover from them.

~

All the same, I would try to console myself about it by thinking that illnesses like that are perhaps to man what ivy is to the oak.

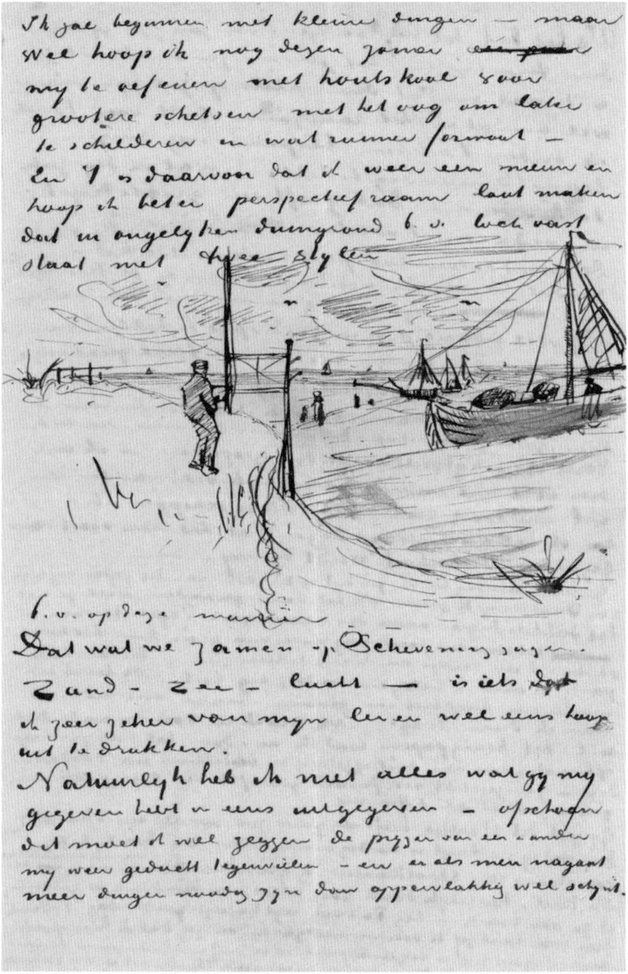

Letter to Theo with sketch of *Beach at Scheveningen with Perspective Frame*, The Hague, 5 August 1882, pen and ink on paper, 21 × 26.6 cm (8⅜ × 10½ in.)

In my mental or nervous fever or madness, I don't know quite what to say or how to name it, my thoughts sailed over many seas.

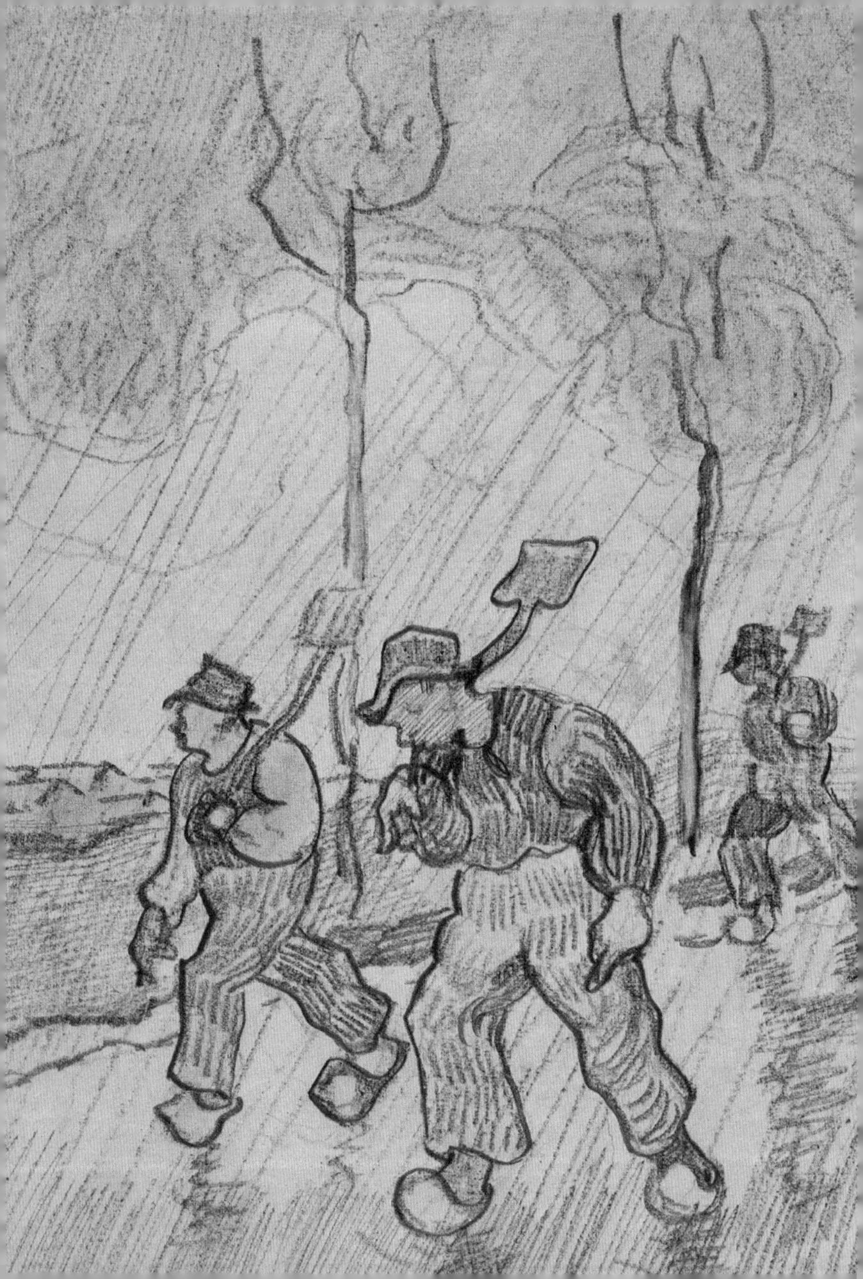

VAN GOGH ON SORROW AND CONSOLATION

It's only in front of the easel while painting that I feel a little of life.

The mental emotions of sadness or disappointments undermine us more than riotous living: us, that is, who find ourselves the happy owners of troubled hearts.

~

How difficult it is to resume one's ordinary life without being absolutely too demoralized by the certainty of unhappiness.

~

However, I know quite well that recovery comes, if one is brave, from inside, through the great resignation to suffering and death, through the abandonment of one's own will and one's self-love.

~

My dear friend, to make of painting what the music of Berlioz and Wagner has been before us...
a consolatory art for distressed hearts!

My word, these anxieties... who can live in modern life without catching his share of them?

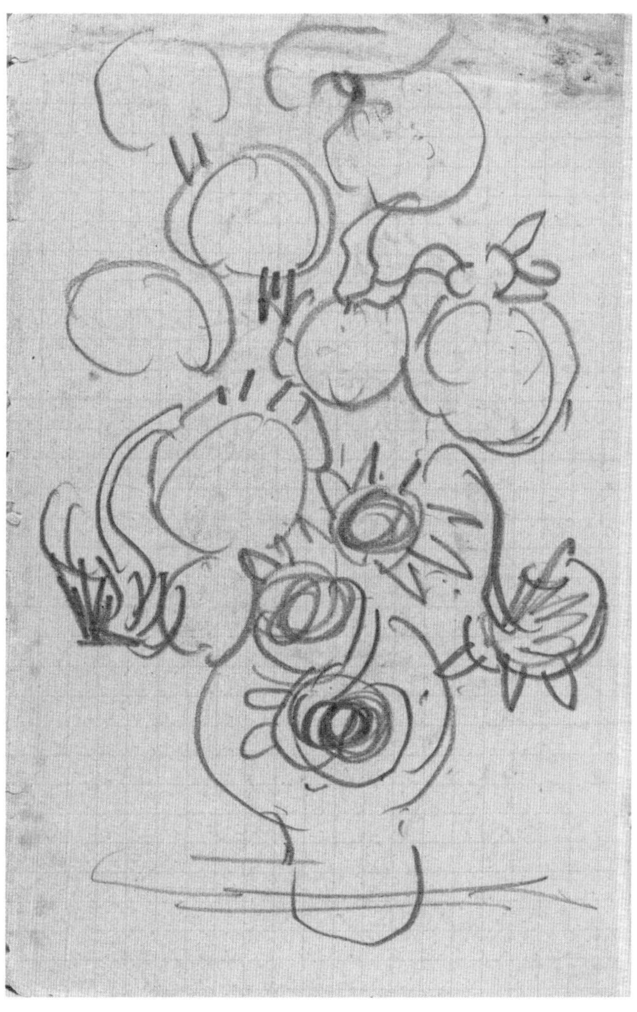

Sunflowers, 1890, pencil on paper, 13.4 × 8.5 cm (5⅜ × 3⅜ in.)

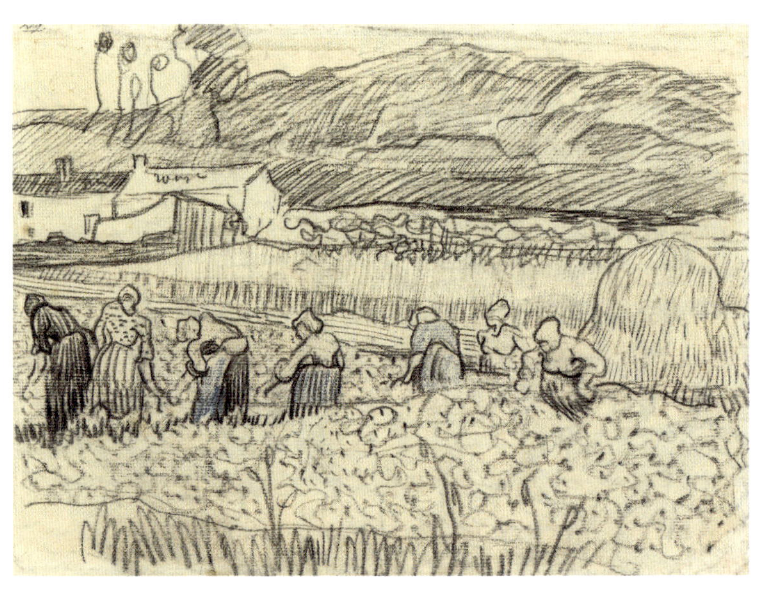

Landscape with Peasant Women Harvesting, 1890, crayon on paper, 23.8 × 31.2 cm (9⅜ × 12⅜ in.)

As an artist one is merely a link in a chain, and whether you find or you don't find, you can console yourself with that.

Grief mustn't
build up in our
souls like the
water of a swamp.

The best consolation, if not the only remedy, is, it still seems to me, profound friendships, even if these have the disadvantage of anchoring us in life more solidly than may appear desirable to us in the days of great suffering.

~

[...] dimly on the horizon, here it comes to me nevertheless – hope – that intermittent hope that has sometimes consoled me in my lonely life.

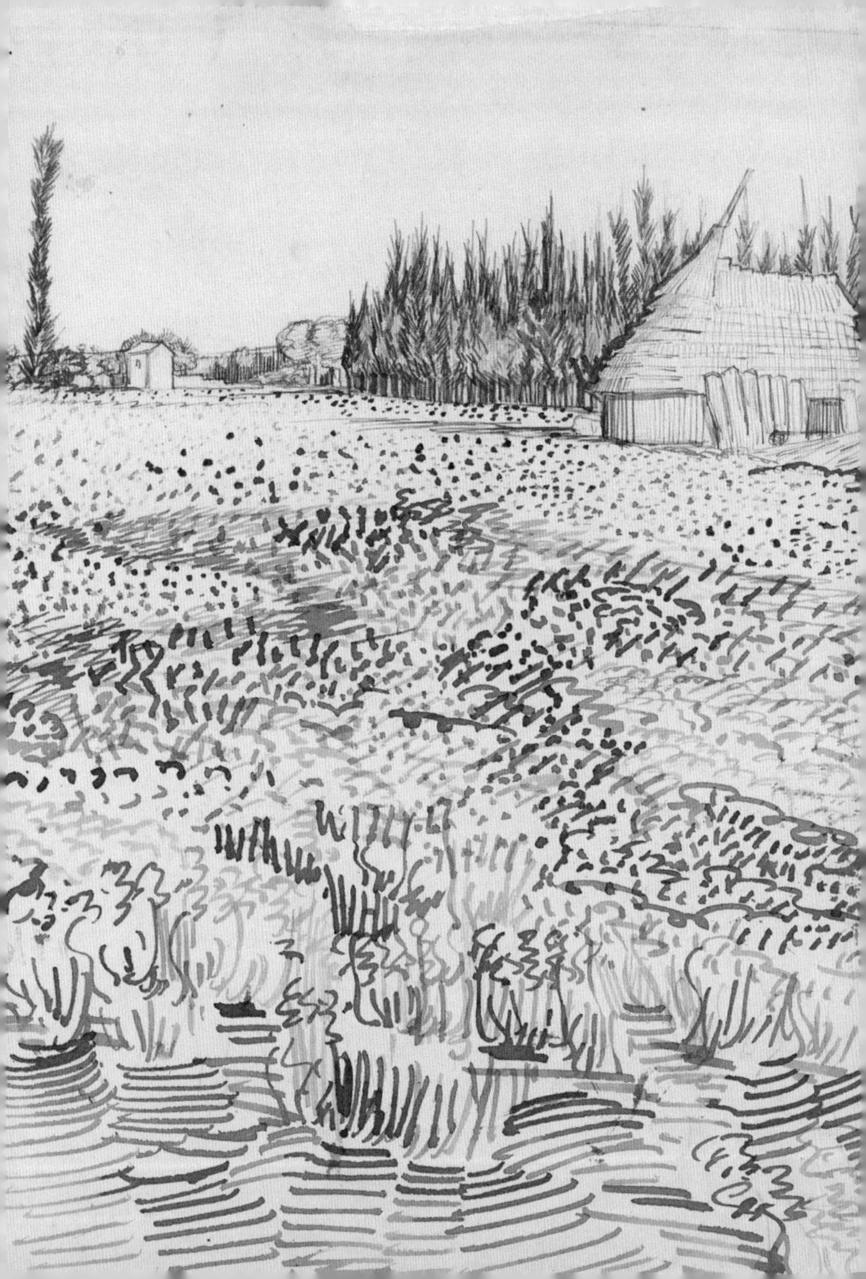

VAN GOGH ON LIFE

It's not good to know only one thing; it stultifies one. One shouldn't rest until one also knows the opposite.

For the great doesn't happen through impulse alone, and is a succession of little things that are brought together.

~

Even if one sometimes feels a sort of decline, the point is nevertheless to revive and have courage, even though things don't turn out as one first thought.

~

What moulting is to birds, the time when they change their feathers, that's adversity or misfortune, hard times, for us human beings.

~

I try to avoid everything that might relate to heroism and martyrdom, in short I try not to take lugubrious things lugubriously.

But even as we stray we sometimes find the track anyway, and there's something good in all movement.

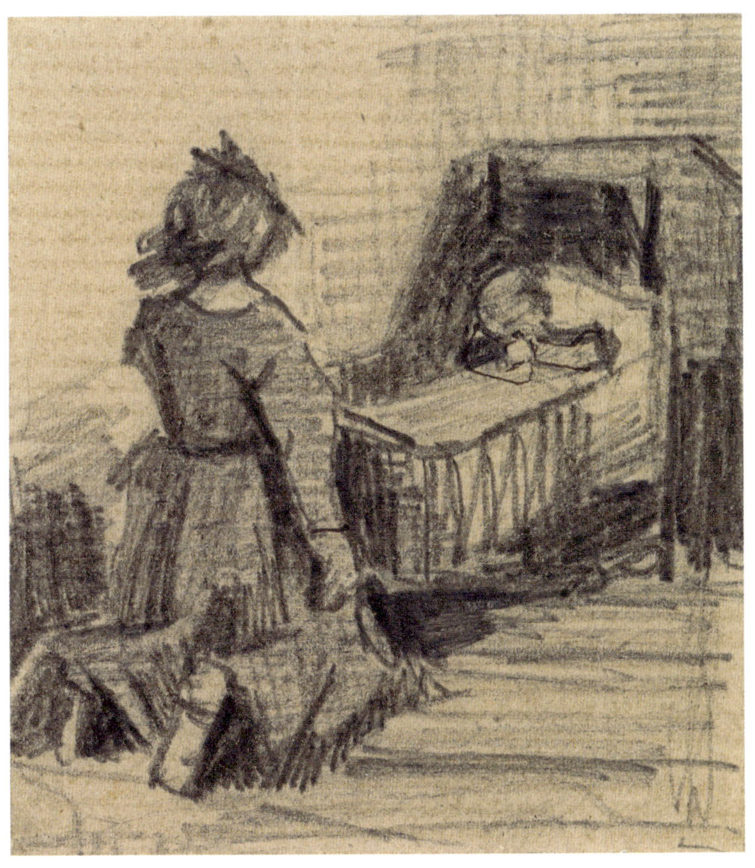

Sketch of *Girl Kneeling by a Cradle*, enclosed in a letter to Theo, The Hague, 18 March 1883, pencil, pen and ink on paper, 7.2 × 6.4 cm (2⅞ × 2⅝ in.)

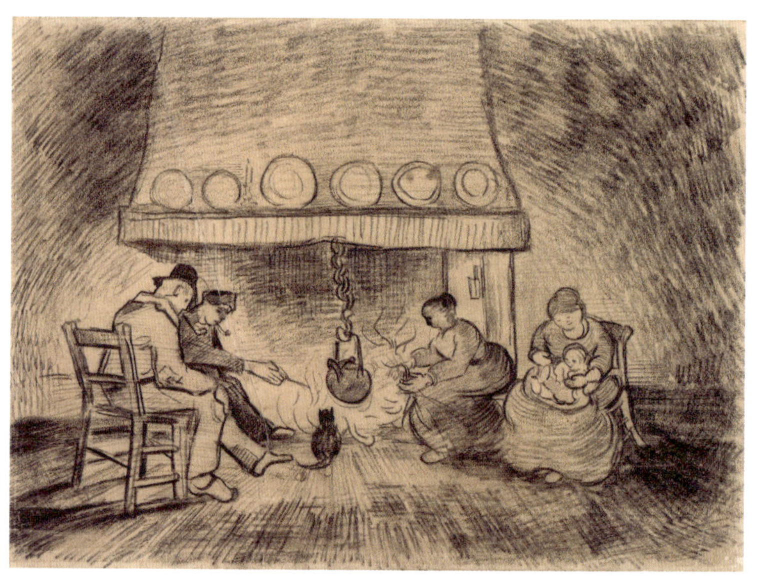

Figures by the Fireplace, 1890, chalk on paper, 23.8 × 31.6 cm (9⅜ × 12½ in.)

To know how to suffer without complaining, that's the only practical thing, that's the great skill, the lesson to learn, the solution to life's problem.

But there — we have to cut our coat according to our cloth, although it's a great shame that there isn't a little more cloth.

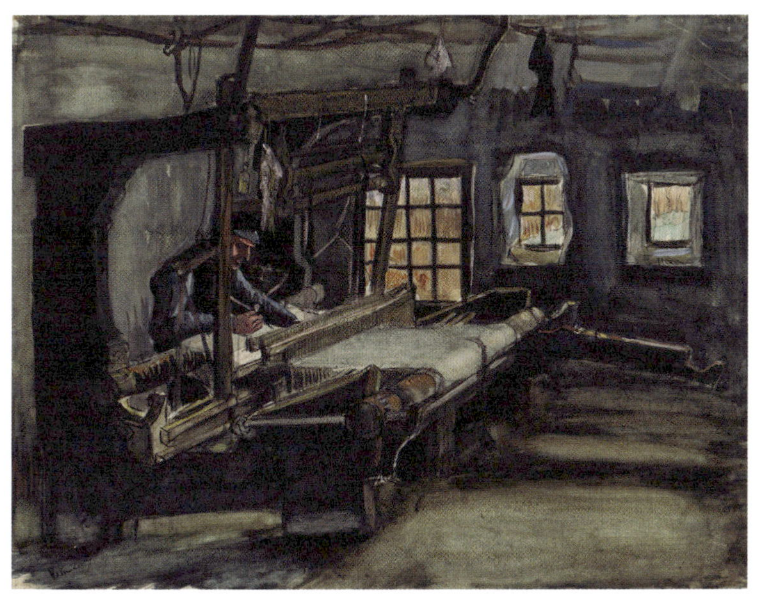

Weaver, 1883–84, pencil, watercolour, pen and ink on paper, 35.5 × 44.6 cm (14 × 17⅝ in.)

The conscience is a man's compass, and although the needle deviates sometimes [...], one must nevertheless do one's best to set one's course by it.

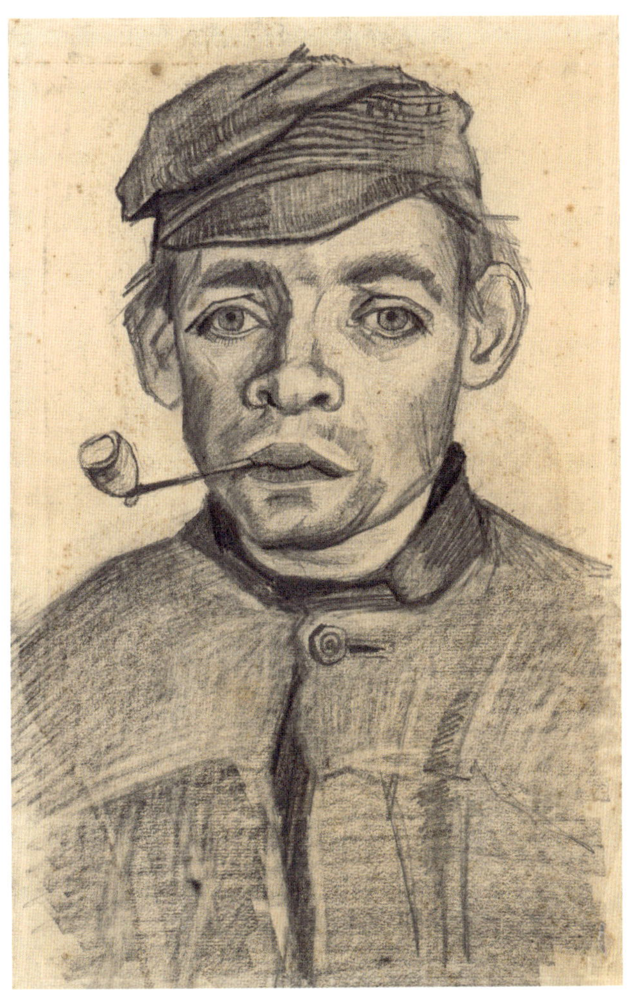

Head of a Young Man with a Pipe, 1884–85, pencil on paper, 33.3 × 20.7 cm (13⅛ × 8¼ in.)

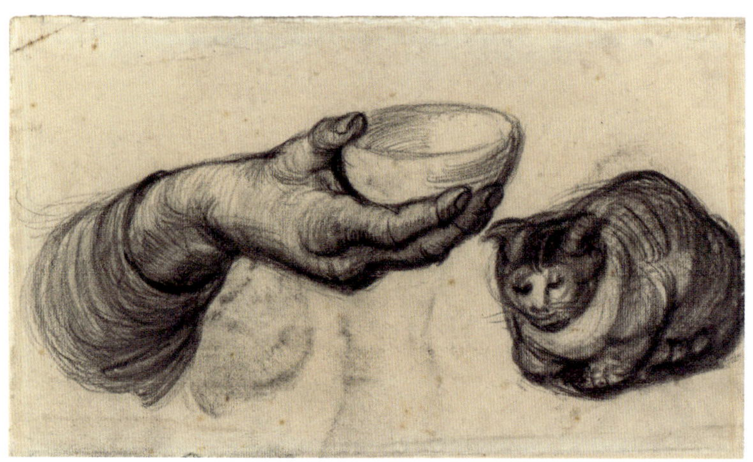

Hand with a Bowl, and a Cat, 1885, chalk on paper, 21.2 × 34.4 cm (8⅜ × 13⅝ in.)

It's certainly true that it is better to be fervent in spirit, even if one accordingly makes more mistakes, than narrow-minded and overly cautious.

Someone who strives for feeling in his work must first feel and live with his heart.

I'm concerned with the world only in that I have a certain *obligation* and *duty*, as it were – because I've walked the earth for 30 years – to leave a certain souvenir in the form of drawings or paintings in gratitude.

~

Holding on to the present and not letting it pass by without managing to get something out of it – now that's what I believe duty is.

~

Like me [...] who can count so many years in my life when I completely lost all inclination to laugh [...] I for one need above all just to have a good laugh.

Success is sometimes the outcome of a whole string of failures.

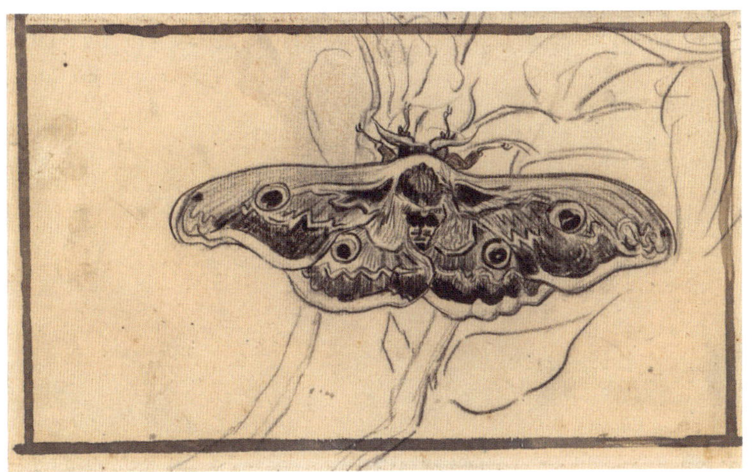

Giant Peacock Moth, 1889, chalk, pen and brush and ink on paper, 16.3 × 24.2 cm (6½ × 9⅝ in.)

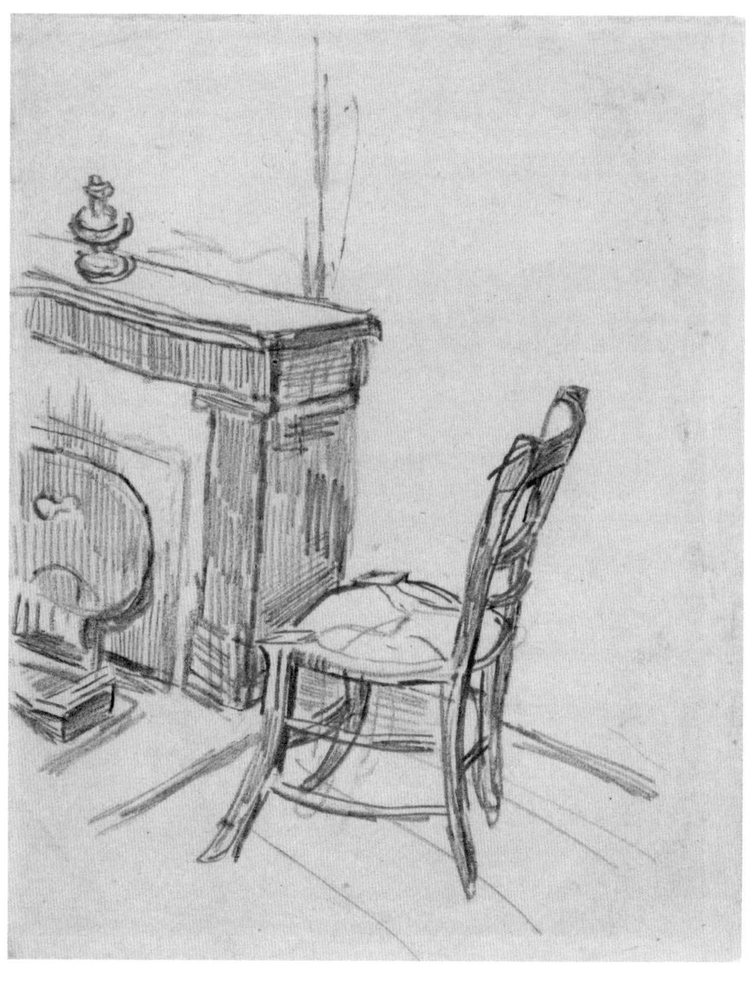

Chair by a Fireplace, 1890, pencil and chalk on paper, 32.5 × 25.1 cm (12⅞ × 10 in.)

Books and reality and art are the same kind of thing for me.

I say it again
— work *against*
indifference —
perseverance isn't
easy — but things
that are easy
mean little.

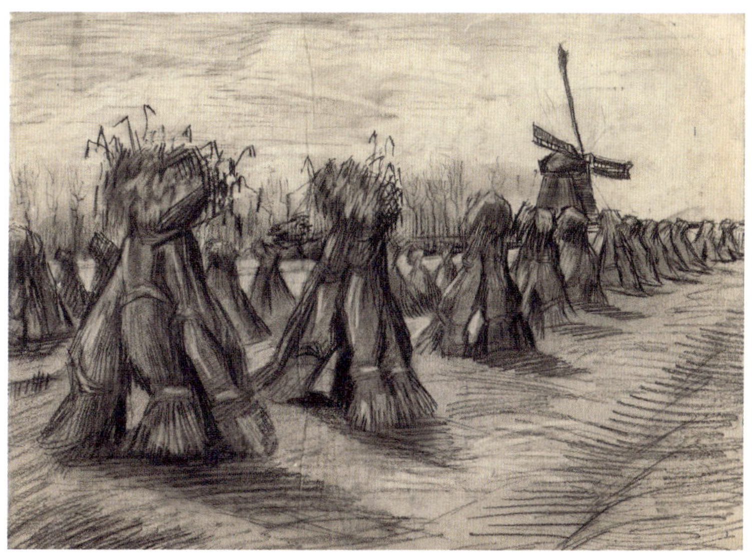

Stooks and a Mill, 1885, chalk on paper, 44.3 × 56.3 cm (17½ × 22¼ in.)

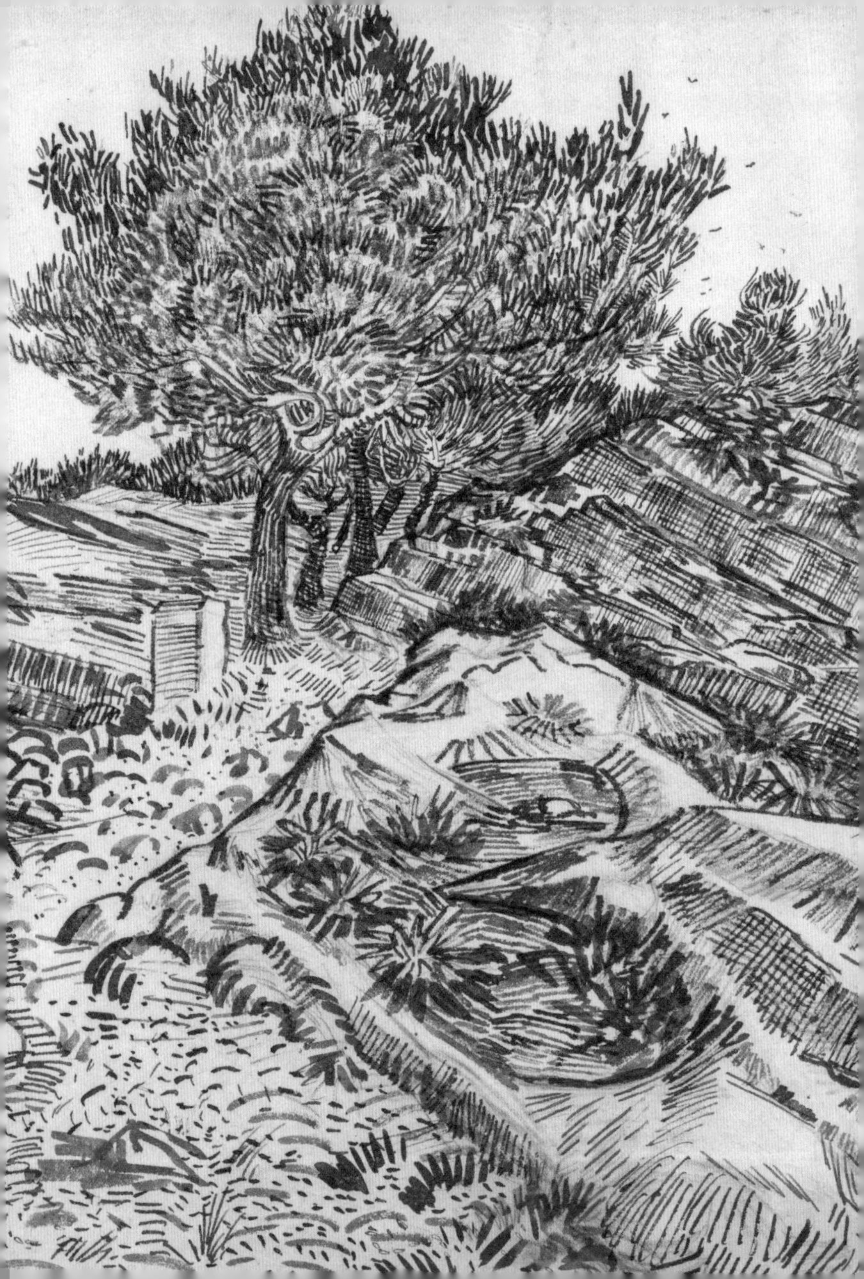

VAN GOGH
ON
SPIRITUALITY

A person who
doesn't feel small –
who doesn't realize
that he's a speck –
what a fundamental
mistake he makes.

That rakes up the eternal question: is *life* visible to us in its entirety, or before we die do we know of only one hemisphere?

~

Life is the same as drawing: sometimes one has to act quickly and resolutely, tackle things with willpower, take care that the broad outlines appear with lightning speed. It's no use hesitating or doubting [...]

~

I'm thinking more and more that we shouldn't judge the Good Lord by this world, because it's one of his studies that turned out badly.

~

Yet if one has a need for something great, something infinite, something in which one can see God, one needn't look far.

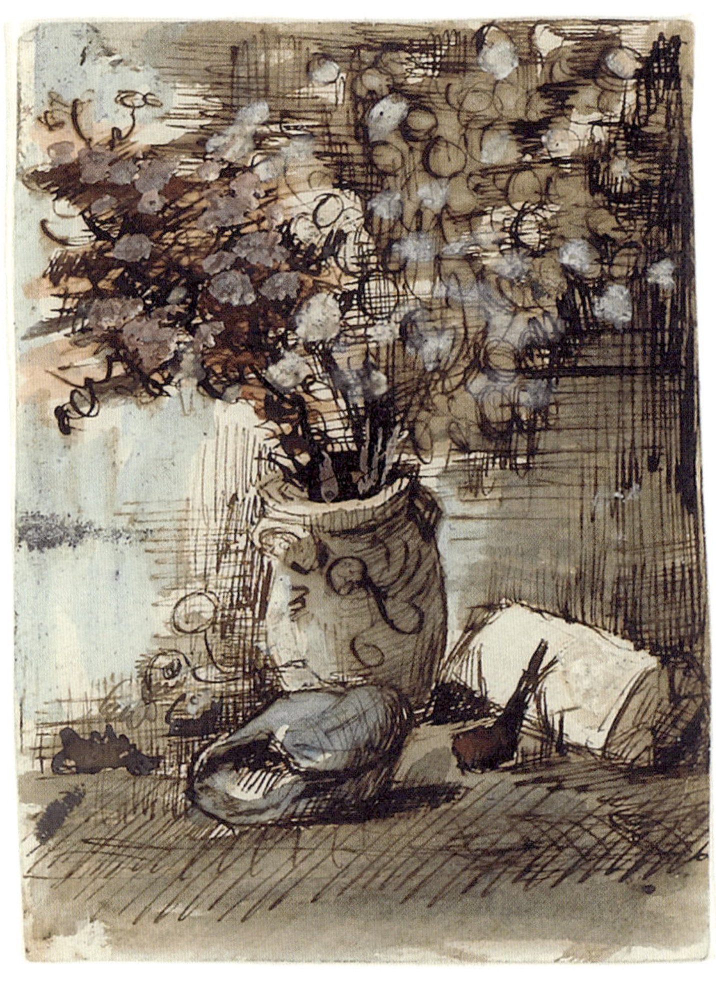

Sketch of *Honesty in a Vase*, enclosed in a letter to Theo, Nuenen, 6 April, 1885, pen and ink, watercolour, gouache on paper, 7.8 × 5.8 cm (3⅛ × 2⅜ in.)

I'm always inclined
to believe that
the best way of
knowing God is
to love a great deal.

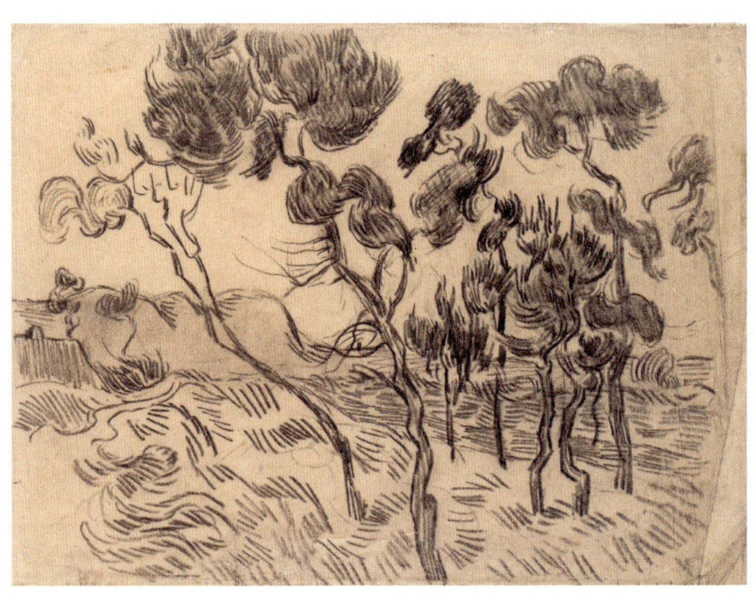

Landscape with Pine Trees, 1889, chalk on paper, 25 × 32.5 cm (9⅞ × 12⅞ in.)

The drama of a
storm in nature,
the drama of
sorrow in life,
is the best.

My dear fellow – let's not forget that small emotions are the great captains of our lives, and that these we obey without knowing it.

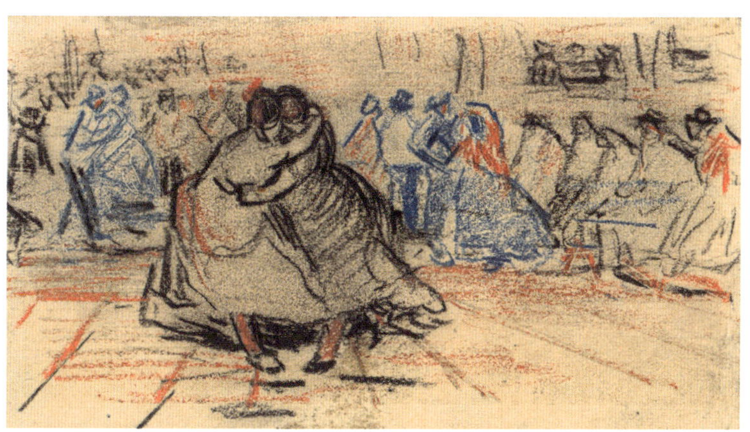

Couple Dancing, 1885, chalk on paper, 9.2 × 16.3 cm (3⅝ × 6½ in.)

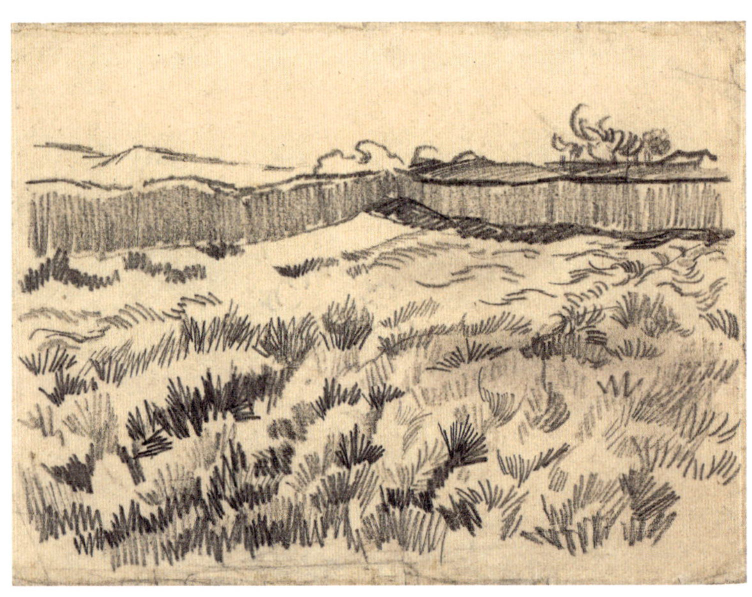

The Walled Wheatfield, 1890, pencil on paper, 25.4 × 32.7 cm (10 × 12⅞ in.)

What else can one do, thinking of all the things whose reason one doesn't understand, but gaze upon the wheatfields.

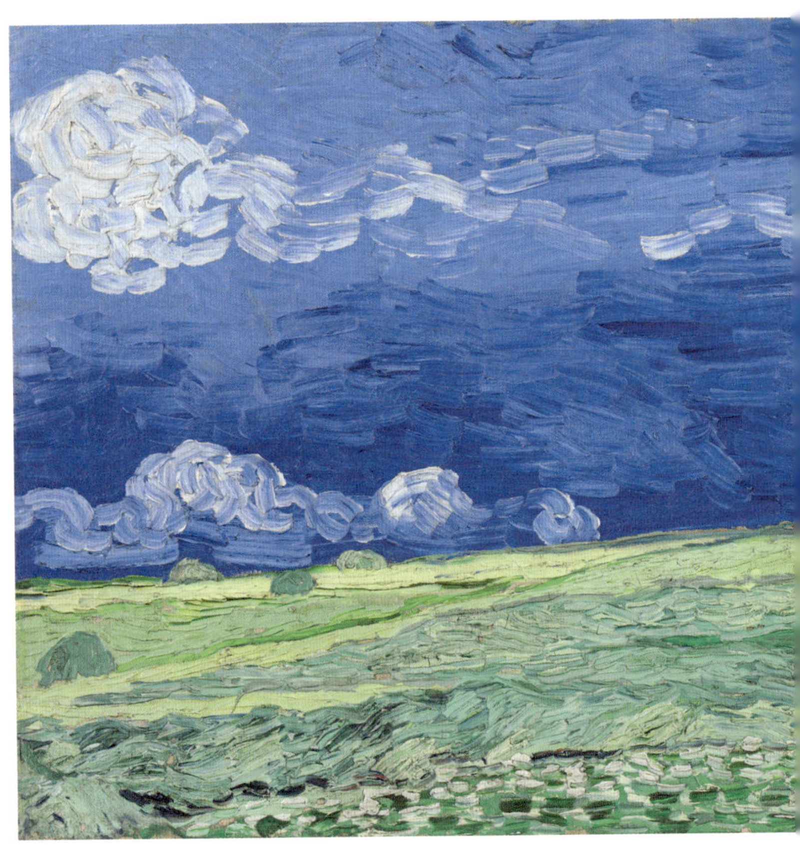

Wheatfield under Thunderclouds, 1890, oil on canvas, 50.4 × 101.3 cm (19⅞ × 40 in.)

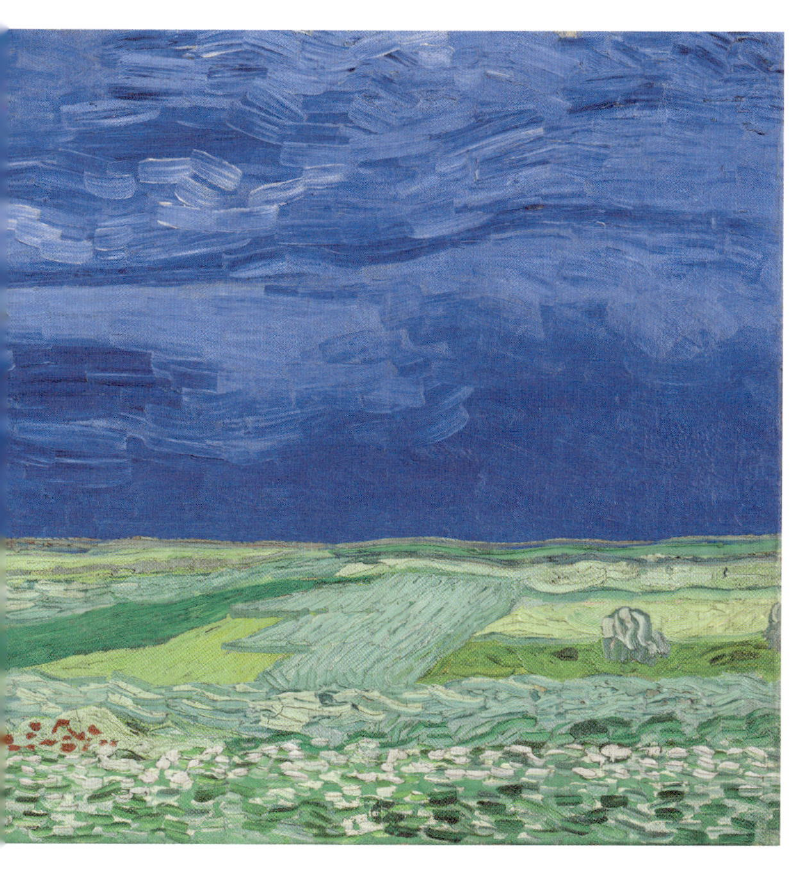

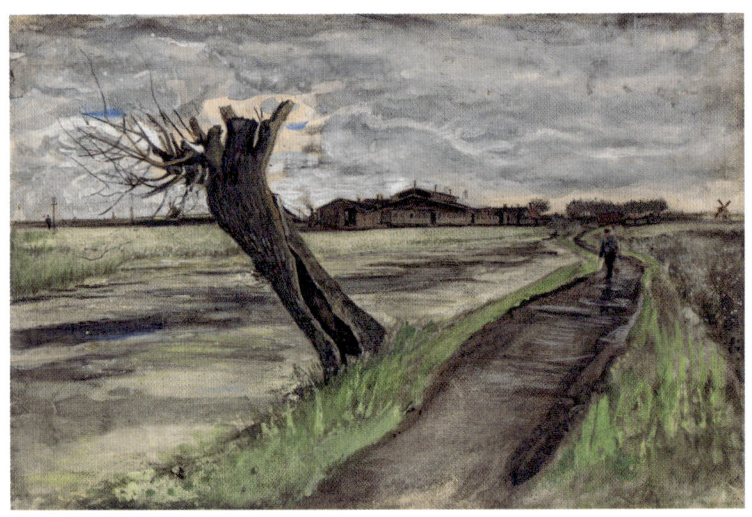

Pollard Willow, 1882, pencil, brown ink, watercolour, chalk on paper, 38 × 55.8 cm (15 × 22 in.)

Fortunately for me,
I no longer count
at all on any victory,
and in painting
I look for nothing
more than the
means of getting
by in life.

But the sight of the stars always makes me dream in as simple a way as the black spots on the map, representing towns and villages, make me dream.

I feel I have a *raison d'être*! I know that I could be a quite different man! For what then could I be of use, for what could I serve! There's something within me, so what is it!

~

I saw something — deeper, more infinite, more eternal than an ocean — in the expression in the eyes of a baby — when it wakes in the morning and crows — or laughs because it sees the sun shine into its cradle.

~

Painters — to speak only of them — being dead and buried, speak to a following generation or to several following generations through their works. Is that all, or is there more, even? In the life of the painter, death may perhaps not be the most difficult thing.

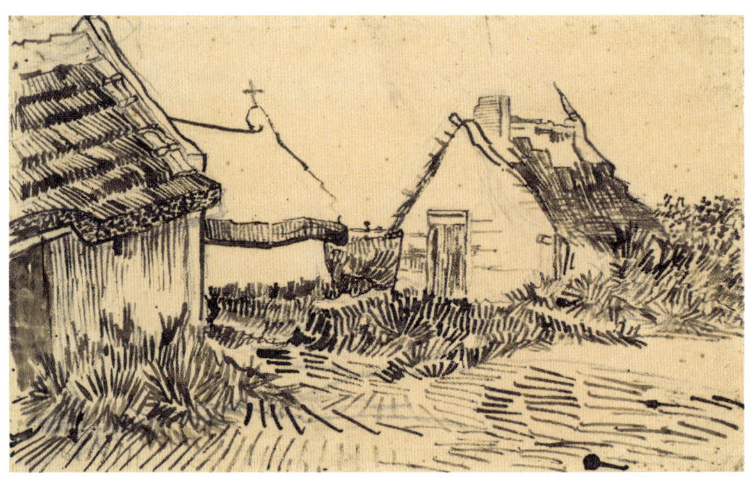

Houses in Les Saintes-Maries-de-la-Mer, 1888, pencil, reed pen and brush and ink on paper, 30.2 × 47.4 cm (12 × 18¾ in.)

Life's 'an odd thing', brother.

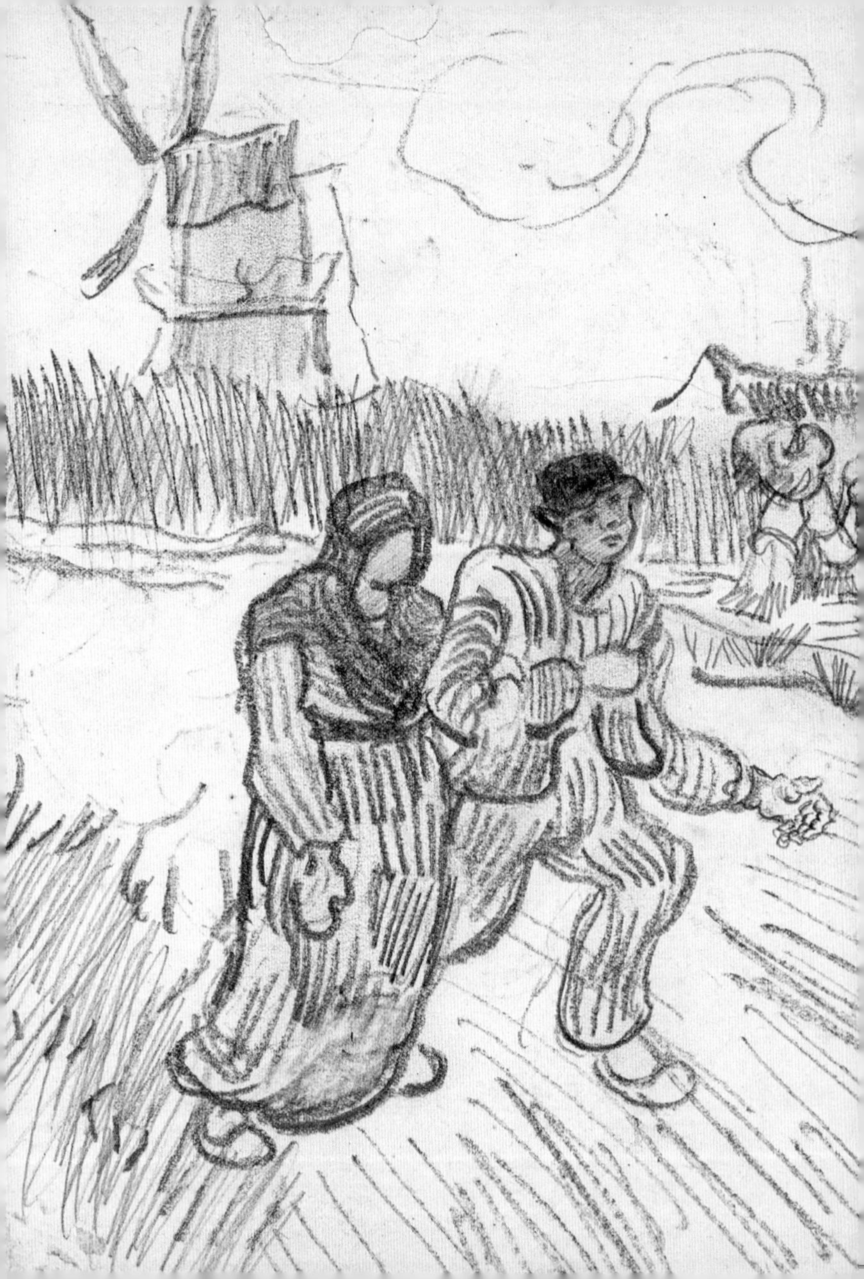

VAN GOGH ON LOVE AND FRIENDSHIP

What a riddle life is,
and love is a riddle
within a riddle.

Loving is in practice not *only* eating strawberries.

~

It is good to love as much as one can, for therein lies true strength, and he who loves much does much and is capable of much, and that which is done with love is well done.

~

For my part, I still continually have the most impossible and highly unsuitable love affairs from which, as a rule, I emerge only with shame and disgrace.

~

I regard love — as I do friendship — not only as a feeling but chiefly as an *action* [...]

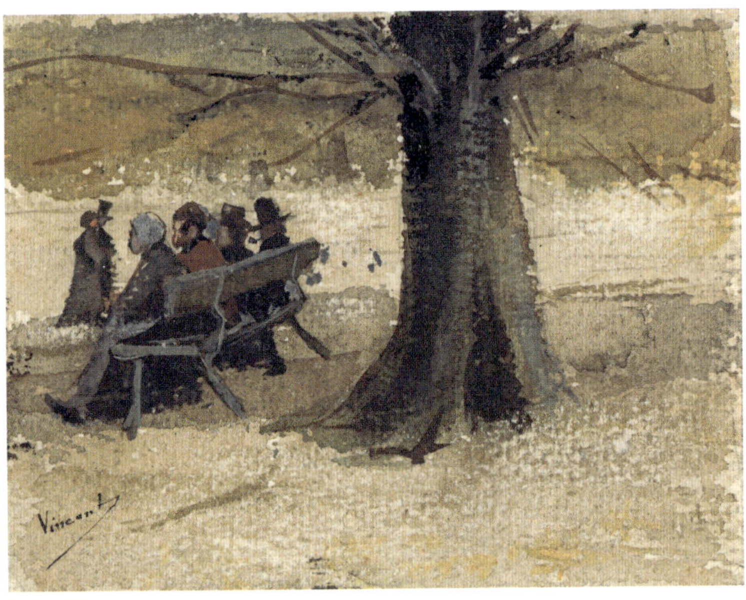

Sketch of *Four People on a Bench* enclosed in a letter to Theo, The Hague, 11 September 1882, pen and ink and watercolour on paper, 9.4 × 11.8 cm (3¾ × 4¾ in.)

If you wake up in the morning and you're not alone and you see in the twilight a fellow human being, it makes the world so much more agreeable.

What keeps us working is friendship for one another and love of nature.

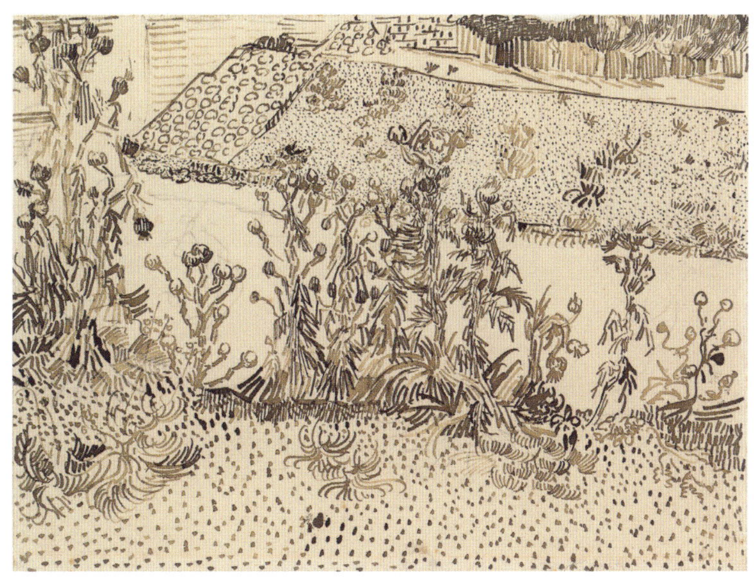

Thistles by the Roadside, 1888, pencil, pen and reed pen and ink on paper, 24.4 × 32 cm (9⅝ × 12⅝ in.)

J'ai bien envie de t'écrire une lettre
exprès que tu pourras leur faire lire
pour ~~leur~~ expliquer encore une fois
pourquoi je crois moi au midi pour
l'avenir et le présent.
Et pour dire en même temps combien
je crois qu'on a raison de voir dans
le mouvement impressioniste une
tendance vers les choses grandes
et non pas seulement une école
qui se bornerait à faire des expériences
optiques. Ainsi pour ceux qui font
alors de la peinture d'histoire ou au moins
l'ont faite dans le temps s'il y a des bien
mauvais peintres d'histoire comme Delaroche et
Delort n'en a t'il pas également des bons
comme Eug Delacroix et Meissonier.
Enfin puisque décidemment j'ai l'intention
de ne pas peindre au moins durant 3 jours
peut être m'y reposerai je en t'écrivant et à
eux en même temps. Car tu sais que cela
m'intéresse assez l'influence qu'aura l'impressionisme
sur les peintres hollandais et sur les amateurs
hollandais

Letter to Theo with sketch of *Row of Cypresses with a Couple Strolling* ('The poet's garden'), Arles, 21 October 1888, pen and ink on paper, 9 × 13.4 cm (3⅝ × 5⅜ in.)

I can't live without love, without a woman. I wouldn't care a fig for life if there wasn't something infinite, something deep, something real.

People who do
nothing other
than be in love are
perhaps more serious
and holier than
those who sacrifice
their love and their
heart to an idea.

Love always causes trouble, that's true, but in its favour, it energizes.

~

The love between brothers is a great support in life, that is an age-old truth.

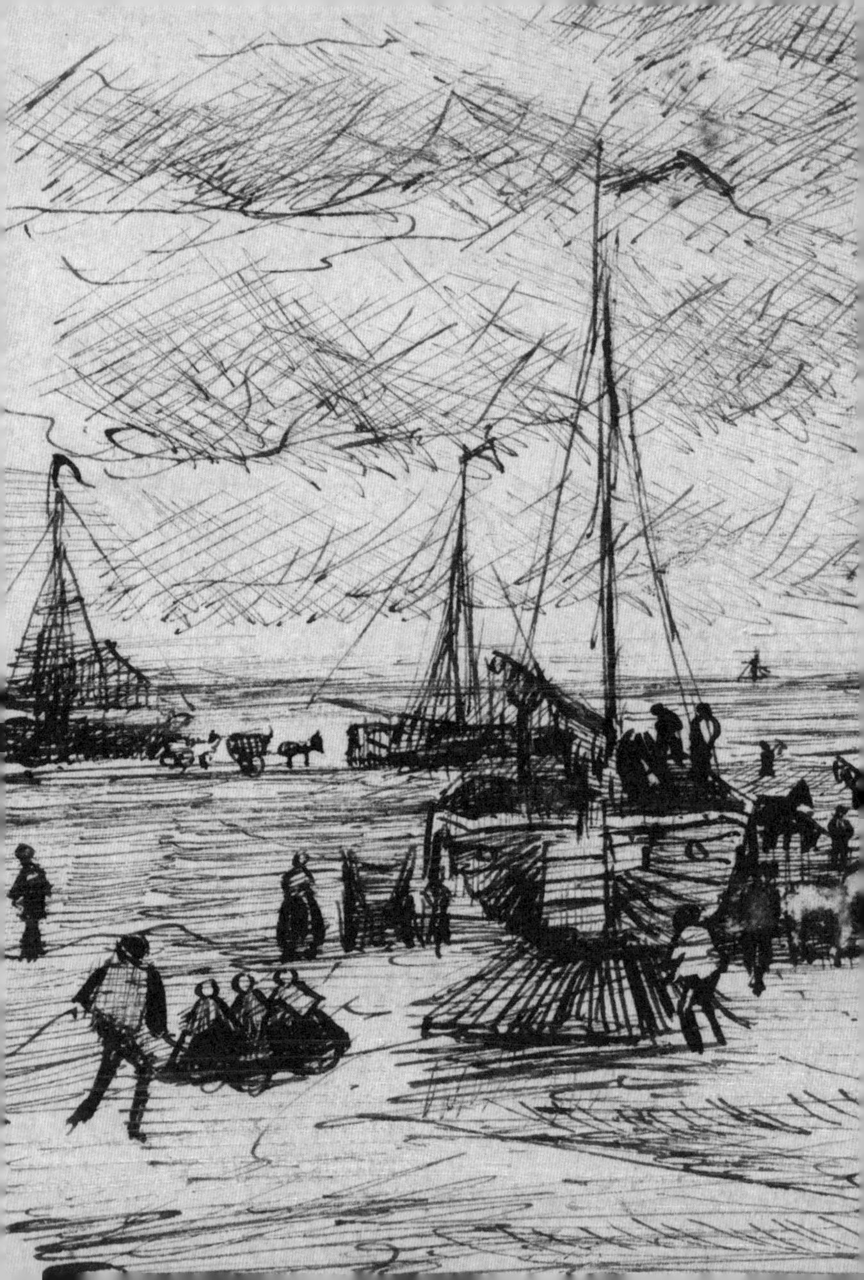

VAN GOGH ON THE FUTURE

I don't know the future, Theo — but — I do know the eternal law that everything changes.

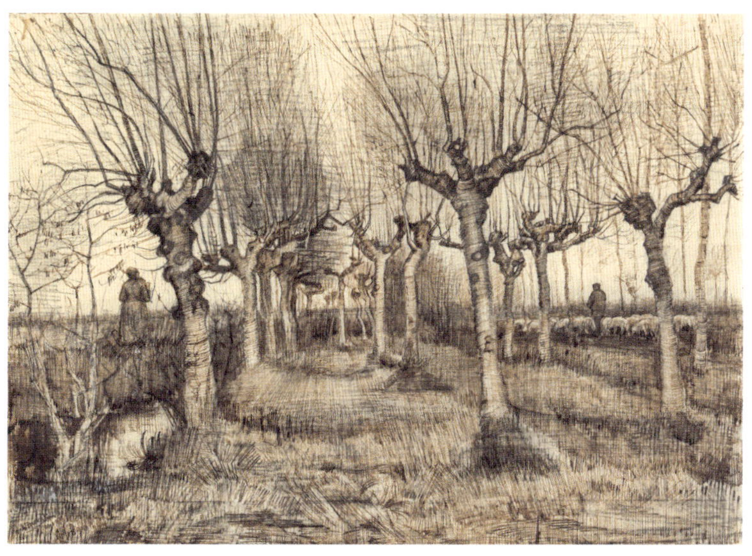

Pollard Birches, 1884, pencil, pen and ink, watercolour on paper, 39.5 × 54.2 cm (15⅝ × 21⅜ in.)

Hoping for better times mustn't be a feeling but a doing something in the present.

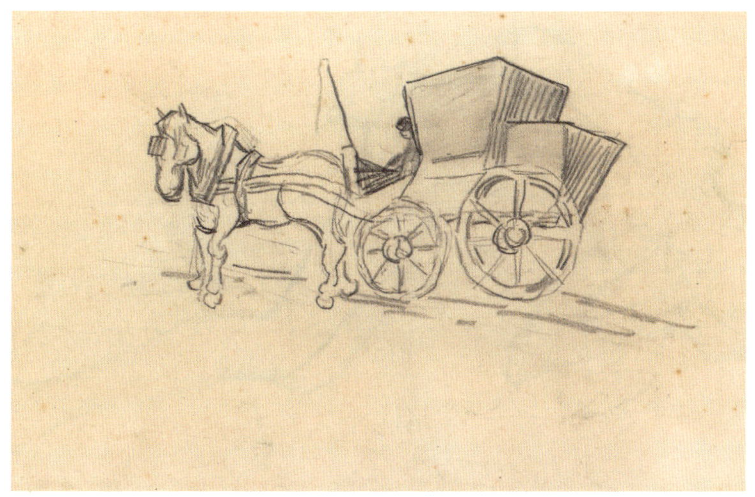

Horse and Carriage, 1890, pencil on paper, 26.9 × 43.7 cm (10⅝ × 17¼ in.)

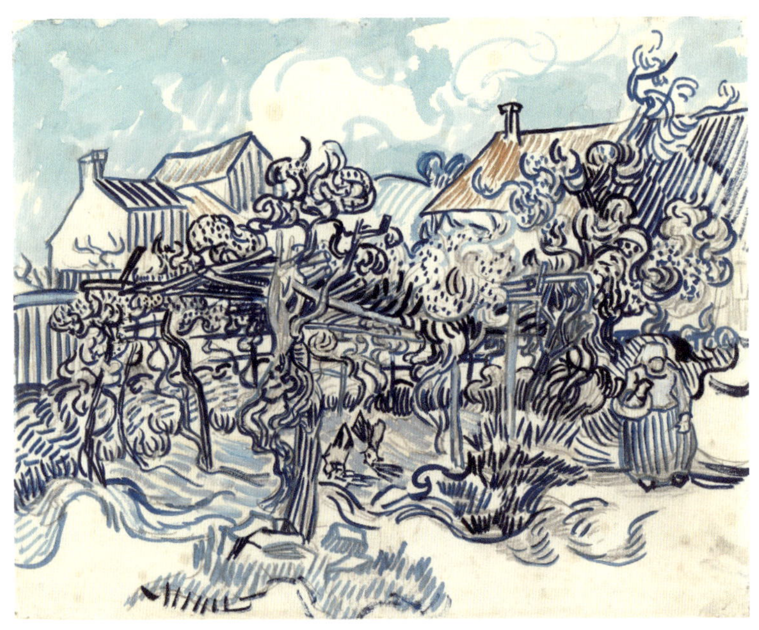

Old Vineyard with Peasant Woman, 1890, pencil, brush and oil paint and watercolour on paper, 44.3 × 54 cm (17½ × 21⅜ in.)

There's an art in the future and it will surely be so beautiful and so young that, really, if at present we leave it our own youth, we can only gain in tranquillity.

It's not in black that I see the future, but I see it bristling with many difficulties, and at times I wonder if these won't be stronger than I am.

~

Providence is such a strange thing, and I tell you that I definitely don't know what to make of it.

~

I believe in the absolute necessity of a new art of colour, of drawing and – of the artistic life. And if we work in that faith, it seems to me that there's a chance that our hopes won't be in vain.

We must be more faithful to the modern than to the old. Looking back at the old is fatal.

SOURCES

The quotes, and the letters from which they have been selected, are available on the website www.vangoghletters.org and in *Vincent van Gogh – The Letters* (6 vols), edited by Leo Jansen, Hans Luijten and Nienke Bakker.

Translation of Van Gogh's letters: Michael Hoyle (general editor)
Translations from the Dutch: Lynne Richards, John Rudge, Diane Webb
Translations from the French: Sue Dyson, Imogen Forster

All quotes are from the following letters (page references are followed by bracketed numbers which refer to the letter numbers on www.vangoghletters.org and in *Vincent van Gogh – The Letters*):

1 (17), 14 (224), 15 (680), 15 (898), 15 (534), 15 (626), 16 (805), 19 (678), 20 (549), 23 (291), 24 (148), 26 (691), 28 (464), 28 (599), 29 (236), 32 (678), 35 (193), 36 (537), 39 (604), 40 (676), 41 (663), 41 (678), 41 (879), 44 (687), 46 (22), 50 (249), 55 (787), 56 (691), 59 (260), 60 (17), 61 (292), 61 (57), 61 (292), 64 (292), 65 (155), 65 (528), 65 (650), 65 (249), 66 (673), 69 (348), 70 (249), 73 (645), 74 (215), 76 (528), 77 (226), 77 (298), 80 (244), 83 (528), 84 (155), 88 (800), 89 (569), 89 (185), 93 (665), 94 (800), 95 (743), 95 (741), 95 (763), 97 (739), 100 (804), 101 (611), 101 (812), 101 (801), 101 (739), 102 (756), 105 (768), 106 (805), 107 (756), 107 (695), 110 (626), 111 (274), 111 (274), 111 (155), 111 (764), 112 (193), 115 (211), 116 (387), 118 (294), 121 (143), 122 (186), 123 (371), 123 (363), 123 (574), 124 (270), 127 (312), 128 (508), 132 (400), 133 (638), 133 (226), 133 (613), 133 (292), 135 (155), 137 (381), 138 (790), 141 (785), 145 (671), 146 (638), 147 (155), 147 (292), 147 (638), 149 (410), 152 (310), 153 (187), 153 (143), 153 (574), 153 (312), 155 (193), 156 (811), 159 (193), 160 (574), 161 (434), 161 (111), 164 (515), 166 (363), 169 (611), 170 (602), 170 (574), 170 (585), 171 (187)

ILLUSTRATIONS

All letters and artworks: Van Gogh Museum, Amsterdam (Vincent van Gogh Foundation); apart from *Van Gogh's Chair*, 1888, oil on canvas, 91.8 × 73 cm (36 ¼ × 28 ¾ in.): The National Gallery, London/Scala, Florence.

Endpapers: *The Bedroom*, 1888, oil on canvas, 72.4 × 91.3 cm (25⅝ × 21⅜ in.)

Page 2: *Self-portrait with Grey Felt Hat*, 1887, oil on cotton, 44.5 × 37.2 cm (17⅝ × 14¾ in.)

Page 12: *Wheatfield under Thunderclouds*, 1890, oil on canvas, 50.4 × 101.3 cm (19⅞ × 40 in.) (detail)

Page 30: *Sunflowers*, 1889, oil on canvas, 95 × 73 cm (37½ × 28¾ in.)

Page 42: *Blossoming Peach Trees*, 1888, chalk and watercolour on paper, 45.4 × 30.7 cm (17⅞ × 12⅛ in.)

Pages 52–53: *Wheatfield with Crows*, 1890, oil on canvas, 50.5 × 103 cm (20 × 40⅝ in.)

Page 62: *Window in the Bataille Restaurant*, 1887, pen and ink, chalk on paper, 54 × 39.8 cm (21⅜ × 15¾ in.)

Page 78: Envelope with sketch of *Five Men and a Child in the Snow*, enclosed in a letter to Theo, The Hague, c. 2 March 1883, chalk and watercolour on part of an envelope, 13.8 × 10.5 cm (5½ × 4¼ in.)

Pages 86–87: *The Potato Eaters*, 1885, oil on canvas, 82 × 114 cm (32⅜ × 4¼ in.)

Page 90: *Van Gogh's Chair*, 1888, oil on canvas, 91.8 × 73 cm (36¼ × 28¾ in.)

Page 98: *Three Men Shouldering Spades on a Road in the Rain*, 1890, pen on paper, 31.8 × 23.9 cm (12⅝ × 9½ in.)

Page 108: *Landscape with Hut*, 1888, pencil, pen and reed pen and ink on paper, 34.8 × 25.7 cm (13¾ × 10⅛ in.) (detail)

Page 130: *The Rock of Montmajour with Pine Trees*, 1888, pencil, pen, reed pen and brush and ink on paper, 49.1 × 61 cm (19⅜ × 24⅛ in.) (detail)

Page 150: *Couple Walking Down a Road*, 1890, pencil on paper, 24.4 × 25.3 cm (9⅝ × 10 in.) (detail)

Page 162: Sketch of *View of the Beach at Scheveningen*, enclosed in a letter to Theo, The Hague, 3 September 1882, pen and ink, chalk, on paper, 8.8 × 6.4 cm (3½ × 2⅝ in.)

BIOGRAPHY

1853
Vincent van Gogh is born on 30 March in Groot-Zundert, the Netherlands, the eldest son of a Protestant minister.

1869–1876
Employed as junior apprentice at branches of Goupil & Cie art dealers. He is eventually fired.

1876
Works as an assistant teacher at boarding schools and later as an assistant preacher in England.

1877
Works as a general assistant in a bookshop in Dordrecht. His faith assumes increasingly fanatical forms.

1877–1878
Lives with his uncle and prepares for the entrance exam to study theology in Amsterdam. Abandons his studies after about a year.

1878–1880
Performs missionary work among poor miners in the Borinage region of Belgium. His six-month appointment is not renewed. Decides at the age of 27 to become an artist and practises by drawing.

1880
Takes drawing lessons at the academy of art in Brussels for a month and befriends the Dutch painter Anthon van Rappard.

1881
Moves in with his parents. Draws mainly peasant figures. His brother Theo supports him financially. Vincent falls in love with his cousin Kee Vos, triggering a fierce conflict with his family.

1881–1883
Takes drawing and painting lessons from Anton Mauve and gets to know other artists as well. Has a studio of his own in The Hague and lives for a prolonged period with the former prostitute Sien Hoornik and her two children.

1883
Spends three months in the Drenthe countryside, where he paints and draws the landscape.

1883–1885
Moves back in with his parents, where he has a small studio. He later rents a room in the village of Neunen. Sets out to become a 'peasant painter' and produces *The Potato Eaters*, his first ambitious painting.

1885–1886
Enrols briefly at the academy of art in Antwerp, but finds it too traditional. Buys his first Japanese prints.

1886–1888
Moves in with his brother Theo in Montmartre. Becomes acquainted with Impressionist and Neo-Impressionist painting in galleries and at exhibitions. Works briefly at Fernand Cormon's studio and befriends Henri de Toulouse-Lautrec and Emile Bernard. Also meets Paul Gauguin. Organizes an exhibition at a restaurant featuring his own work and that of fellow artists.

1888–1889
Moves to Provence in search of calm, a warmer climate and bright colours. Rents the Yellow House, where he hopes to live and work with other artists. Paints a series of canvases to decorate the house, including *Sunflowers* and *The Bedroom*. Lives with Gauguin for two months. Suffers a mental breakdown and cuts off his left ear.

1889–1890
Having suffered repeated episodes of his illness, he has himself admitted to an asylum in Saint-Rémy-de-Provence. His doctor diagnoses a form of epilepsy; it is believed nowadays that he was suffering from psychosis. Has an extra room to use as a studio and produces numerous drawings and paintings between breakdowns, including *Almond Blossom*.

1890
Leaves the asylum in Saint-Rémy and moves to the village of Auvers-sur-Oise, near Paris. He paints a great deal, averaging one canvas a day. Yet the future seems bleak. Shoots himself in the chest with a revolver and dies two days later, on 29 July, with Theo at his side.

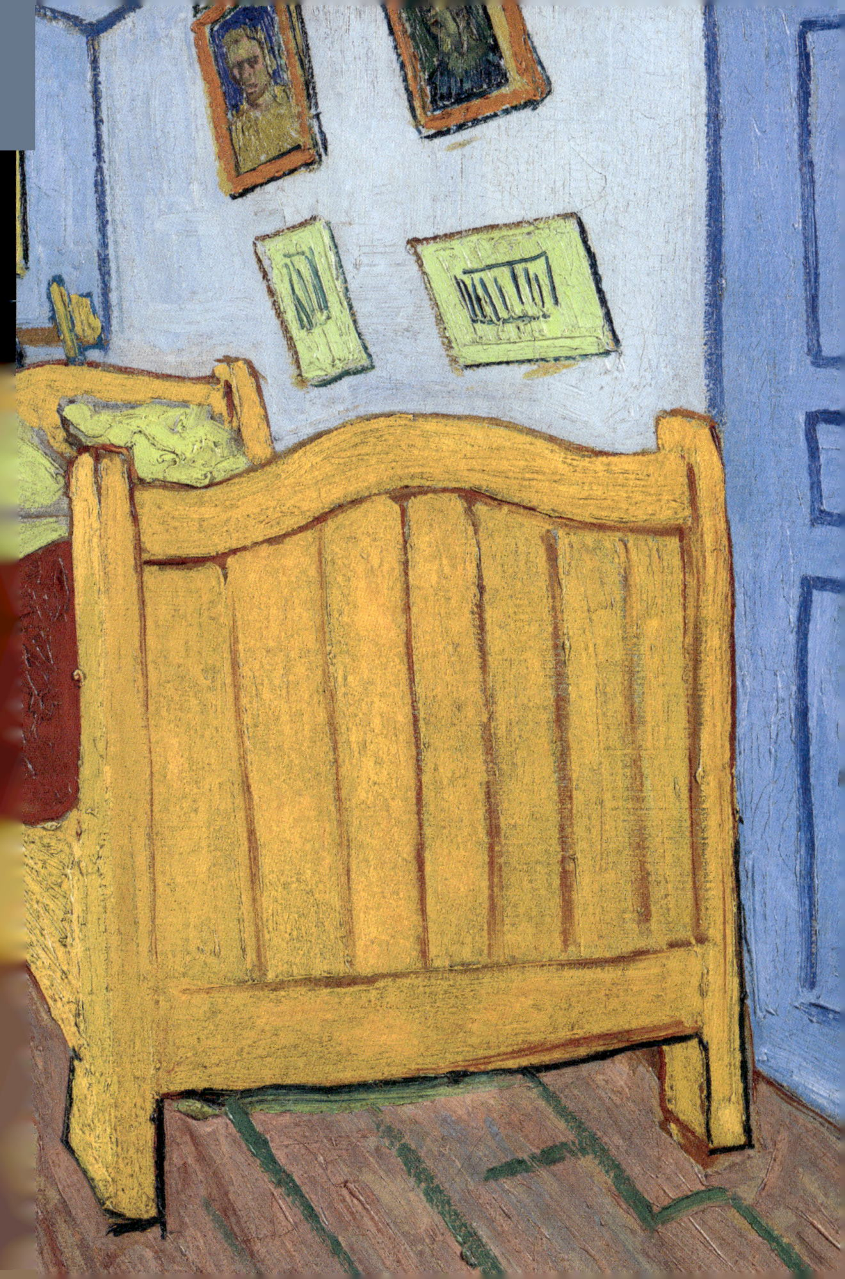

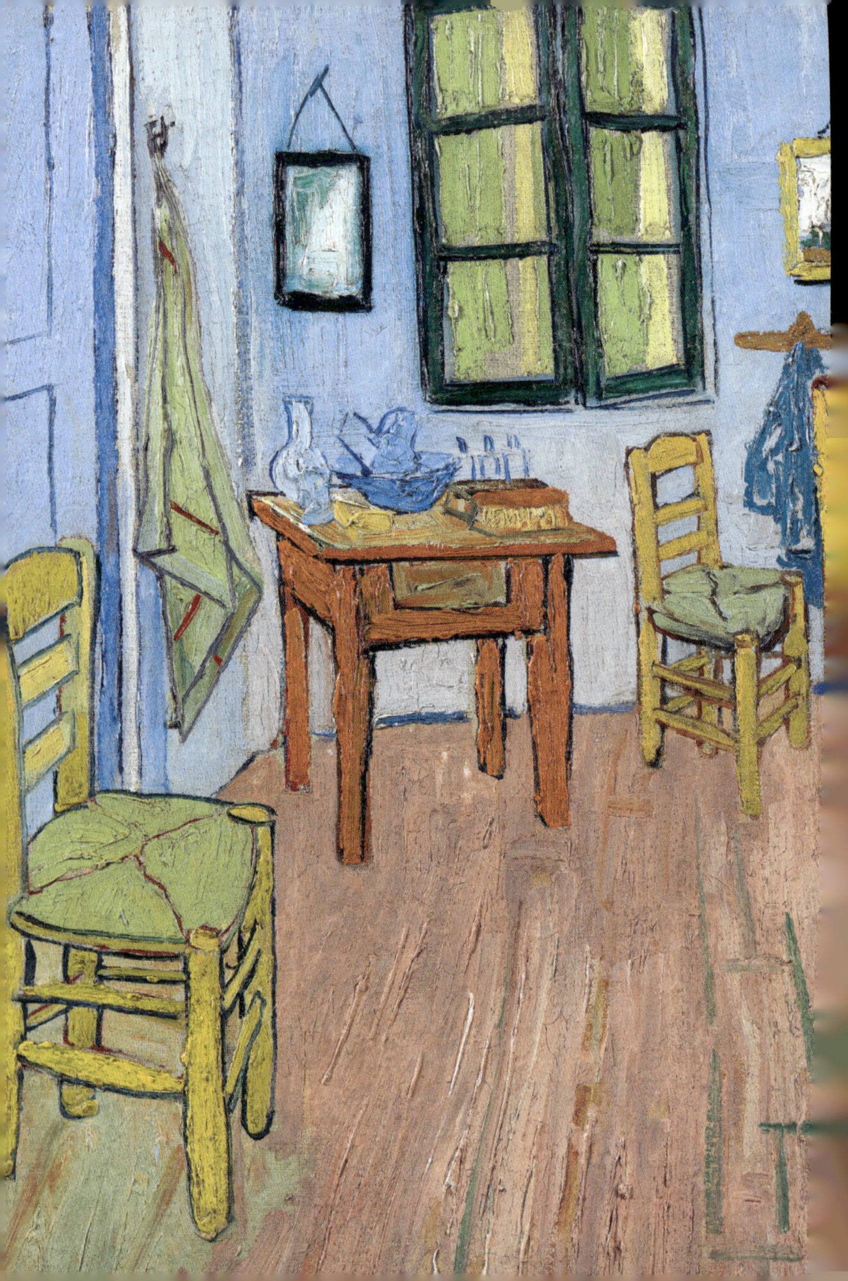